A Short History of Amsterdam

The Westertoren of 1631, after Hedrick de Keyser's design. De Emperor's crown on the Westertoren was the symbol of Amsterdam's self-awareness.

A Short History of Amsterdam

Dr. Richter Roegholt

Bekking & Blitz Publishers b.v., Amersfoort

Bekking & Blitz Uitgevers b. v. Amersfoort

ISBN 9061095522

A Dutch edition of this book is also available, with the title Geschiedenis van Amsterdam in Vogelvlucht.

Cover illustration
Hendrik Corneliz. Vroom, 1566–1640.
The Return to Amsterdam of the second expedition to the East-Indies, 1599.

Translation
Andrew Niemeijer

Graphic design
Ronald Boiten and Irene Mesu, Amersfoort

Lithography
Scanmail, Amersfoort

Contents

AMESTELLEREDAMME
A° 1230
AME
Y

In 1980 Paul Schindeler drew this fantasy of Amsterdam origin for Het Parool.

Chapter 1

A City between Utrecht and Holland 1265–1400

Amsterdam is a city of paradoxes. It is the capital of The Netherlands, but it's seat of government does not reside there. The old town hall is called the Royal Palace. The treaty which signifies the birth of the independent state of The Netherlands is called the treaty of Utrecht. The Dutch royal family (the House of Orange) have their palaces in The Hague, Soestdijk and Apeldoorn, their mausoleum is in Delft. The head offices of the postal service, railway, radio and television are not in Amsterdam. Amsterdam is not the largest port in the country. It has always been a seaport and Rhine harbour, but Amsterdam lies neither on the seacoast or on the river Rhine.

However, no Dutchman has any hesitation in regarding Amsterdam as the capital city. It is the only city in the country that really counts, the epicentre of where things 'are happening'. Moreover, things take place in Amsterdam before they take place anywhere else in Holland. It's where trends in fashion, advertising, literature and art are created, it's the city for the young and ambitious, for those who 'want it all'. And if someone points you to the cultural centres of Laren and Blaricum, Bergen and Groet and faraway Giethoorn, then these cultural hotspots are the derivatives, the outposts of the only great city which sets the tone in Holland – or at least it behaves as though it does – and that city is Amsterdam.

(p. 8)
Detail from Hendrick Cornelisz. Vroom, a Dutch three-master advancing the Sont at Fort Kronberg (1614).

Since Amsterdam came into existence in the thirteenth century it has belonged to various states which constitute the Netherlands, the historical sequence of which reflects the history of this country as a whole. There were paradoxes from the outset of this great city. Nowadays, no one would expect a city could be created in a marshy meadowland surrounded by lakes and riddled by waterways. One of these waterways was the Amstel, a sluggish little river that drained the extremely wet land. The Amstel flowed into the IJ through a broad estuary, and in its turn the IJ also flowed through and estuary into the Zuiderzee. A, Ame or Amer; Ee, Eem or Eems; Ie, IJ or IJssel; they all mean 'aqua', water. In the fist place the Amestelle was the 'stelle' (the dry place) beside the water, a name that signified the transition form the land to the water. 'Amstelland' is therefore a pleonasm. The Amstelland was a dangerous place, for whenever the wind was blowing form the north-east it piled the water up, causing the entire area to be at risk to floods

Government

The region belong to the diocese of Utrecht – the 'Sticht' and was administered in the name of the bishop by liegemen of the Van Aemstel family. This family of knights attempted to found an independent medieval state as a wedge between the diocese of Utrecht and the county of Holland. In 1204 their stronghold in Oudekerk was destroyed by the rebellious Kennemer farmers, who also took the opportunity to pierce

Amsterdam and Amstelland, map by Joost Jansz., a woodcarver in 1575. Amsterdam is encircled by the Kloveniersburgwal, which changes into the Singelgracht. Outside Amsterdam, from left to right, one can see the Diemermeer, the Bijlmermeer, the Oude Meer, the Nieuwe Meer and the Slotermeer. At the bottom left the H.Wech (Heiligeweg) enters the city, the pilgrim's route to the Heilge Stede. At the right, just under Weesp, a line indicates the border between Holland and Sticht (Utrecht). (GAA)

the Amstel dikes. This may have been the reason why the Aemstels established their castle to the west of the mouth of the Amstel. The foundations of this castle were discovered in the Nieuwezijds Kolk in 1994. The supreme authority of our lands was the emperor of Germany.

We can make a guess about the time the Dam was constructed. An agreement exists between Gijsbrecht IV van Aemstel and his brother Willem, provost of the region round Mijdrecht, Wilnis and Kudelstaart, regarding the drainage of his lands into the Amstel. The fact that this had to be regulated indicates that the Amstel was no longer openly linked to the IJ. At the very earliest the Dam could have been constructed in the year 1265, the year that Willem assumed his position. Let's, for the sake of argument, determine the year to be 1270. The dam formed a link in the sea dike from Muiden to Spaarndam. The dam was built quite a way inland, which meant that longer lengths of existing dike had to be strengthened. The advantage to this was that the strengthened dikes provided a place for houses to be built. From the Dam, to the left and right of the river, both dikes went northwards – the present-day Nieuwendijk, which at the end curves left towards Spaarndam; and the present-day Nieuwendijk, and the present-day Warmoesstraat, which at the mouth of the Amstel curves quite sharply to the south-east, and which to this day bears the name 'Zeedijk'. Even now it is still clearly visible that these streets, which partly carry the name 'dijk' (dike), are higher than their surroundings.

Occupation and trade

Here lay the fruitful foundations of Amsterdam. The ships needed to discharge their cargoes at the Dam. There were stopovers, which meant a hostelry was needed, allowing entertainment and trade to flourish. A market came into existence, the open water of the Damrak was the natural harbour and the people lived on and behind the dikes. We owe what we know of these inhabitants of Amsterdam to the excavations carried out by the city's archaeological service. They were fishermen,

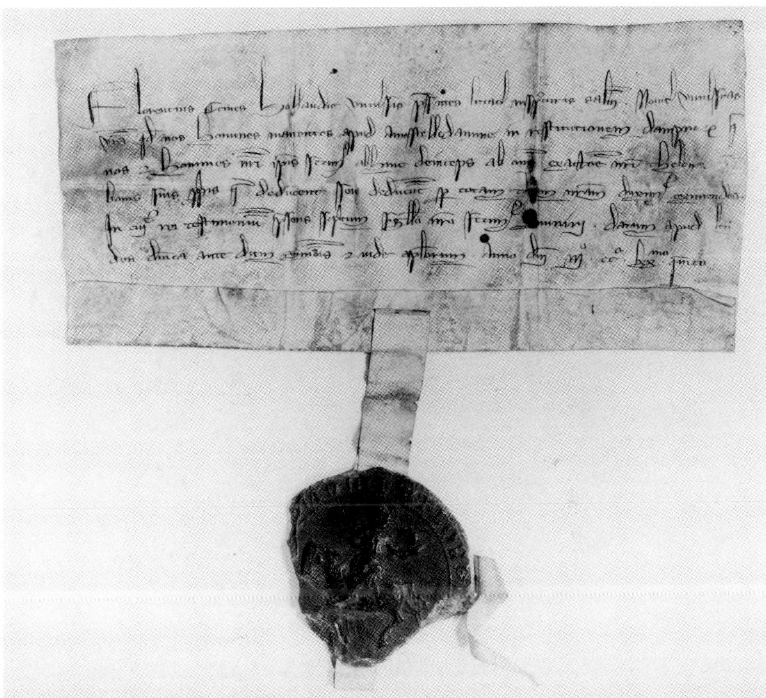

The 1275 Privilege. (GAA)

craftsmen and traders and, naturally, agriculture and cattle farming were important as well. It has been calculated that before 1275 there were some hundred houses sheltering perhaps some 500 people. A layer of clay consolidated the peaty ground and the houses were built of plaited willow osiers, which were thickly smeared with clay. In this way so-called 'terps' (mounds or knolls) were created. There was a hearth made of red bricks called 'kloostermoppen' (Roman bricks). Remains have been found which indicate the existence of a forge and of a needle maker, and spinning and weaving must have taken place. This leads one to conclude that there was also some trading activity, for the blacksmith needed his iron ore, which came from Germany. Because the soft peaty ground was continually settling every five years or so the inhabitants had to raise their houses. Archaeologists have found as many as eight hearths in layers above each other, the oldest of which is six metres below the present day street level.

This little settlement by the Dam on the Amstel, which belonged to Utrecht, was, nevertheless, important enough for Floris V, count of the province of Holland, to desire its favour. A early as 1275 Floris granted the 'luyden woonende tot Aemstelledamme', (people living in Amsterdam), the right to trade in Holland without having to pay tolls. In doing this he undermined the authority of the bishop of Utrecht, and at the same time the power of the ambitious Gijsbrecht van Aemstel. By bestowing this celebrated toll privilege Floris V actually provided the first page of written history of Amsterdam. What was it all about, there at the mouth of the Amstel, that handful of little people? A people, a market and an harbour, armed with a powerful privilege. The world would hear from them.

'Farewell my Amsterdam/Expect another Lord.'

Gijsbrecht IV did not succeed in his scheme to become a third power between Utrecht and Holland for the powerful Count of Holland would not allow it. After a successful war against Utrecht in which Gijsbrecht had put himself at the head of the – yet again – rebellious Kennemer farmers, Holland intervened. This was global politics on a small scale. The farmers rushed home because it was harvest time and Count Floris took Gijsbrecht prisoner. At their reconciliation in 1285 Gijsbrecht was forced to agree to become a vassal of Holland and to surrender some of his lands. However, in 1296 he was indirectly involved in the murder of Floris V, and was forced to flee the country. One of his cousins, Jan van Avesnes, succeeded the murdered Floris from faraway Henegouwen.

But the struggle for the future of Amsterdam had not been decided yet. In 1303 Holland's position was threatened by a rapid Flemish invasion, a direct cause of the long battle between Holland and Flanders over the possession of Zeeland. Gijsbrecht's son, Jan van Aemstel, took advantage of this situation by occupying Amsterdam and turning

During digging works at the Niewezijds Kolk in March 1994 a brick foundation was found which might have been part of the Aemstel Castle. (Author's picture)

against Holland. The Flemish, however, were driven back just as quickly as they had invaded, and Jan van Aemstel was forced to surrender Amsterdam again. The city was severely punished, for it was forced to demolish its town walls and destroy its bridges, and consequently lost all its privileges. This 'downfall' of Amsterdam inspired Joost van den Vondel to write his tragedy *Gijsbrecht van Aemstel*. In 'Gijsbrecht' Vondel portrays the city in the width and breadth of his time, including the street- names the people of Amsterdam recognised. The play focuses on the siege of the city and the cunning ploy the enemy used to take Amsterdam. Vondel lets his hero Gijsbrecht escape the burning Amsterdam with the words: "*Farewell my Aemsterland, expect another lord*". In fact, Vondel has amalgamated the histories of both Gijsbrecht IV and his son Jan, who were both in conflict with the powerful Holland, into one tragedy.

Count Willem III of Holland handed Amsterdam temporarily to Gwijde, the Bishop of Utrecht, who, not coincidentally, was Willem the

Third's uncle. However, after the bishop's death in 1317, Amsterdam was definitively incorporated into Holland. After this there was no liegeman between the city and the count. All the privileges Amsterdam had lost in 1304 were restored. The county of Holland was the second political entity under which Amsterdam fell, Holland being preceded only by the bishopric of Utrecht. The arrival of the Henegouwen house to Holland was a step towards the merging of the regions of the Netherlands. Marriage politics and the rights of succession would do their work.

The remarkable thing about the minor wars of the Middle Ages, which are reminiscent of the take-overs and mergers of large companies in modern times, is that you never heard much about the people involved. We can deduce from the periodically flaring rebelliousness of the farmers how badly they were exploited and continually made scapegoats, but there are no witnesses. In 1494 there was a revolt of the farmers which was celled the rise of the 'Cheese and Bread people'. There is a song called the *Kerelslied* which is about this and other uprisings. In the *Kerelslied* the farmers are seen through the eyes of the aristocracy as an unrefined pillaging horde. However, in rebuke of this was the saying which takes the farmers side: '*When Adam was digging and Eve was spinning, where was then the nobleman?*'. The farmers supplied food and clothing whilst the aristocracy had no use whatsoever. The City, that new phenomena of medieval society, plays no part in either texts. To put it clearly, we know nothing of the feelings of the Amsterdammers, nor do we know what side they took, cast as they were between Utrecht, Aemstel and Holland.

Where Lines of Communication Intersect

There are countless towns and cities with '-dam' in their name, or with '-voort' or '-voorde', indicating a place where a river was fordable. But none of these towns and cities has expanded so much as Amsterdam. Here the intersection of lines of communication formed fertile ground for trade and meetings between peoples and cultures.

The Netherlands owes its independence to its geographical position – it controls the mouths of the great rivers. Therefore its powerful neighbours have never successfully subjected it. The Dutch were by nature prepared to maintain the balance of power between their neighbouring countries by forming continually changing alliances. The region of Holland profited most from these geographic advantages, and in Holland it was Amsterdam that united these characteristics of the Netherlands and Holland. It was advantageously situated, protected from its enemies by water and marshlands, and always ready and able to play all the others off against each other; the tradition that Amsterdam behaves in a high-handed manner still lives on today.

The age of the crusades (the first crusade began in 1096) had brought Europe into contact with the Middle East, a fairytale world of affluence and refinement. Trading took place, allowing real money to come into circulation. What's more, a need was created for capital and for borrowing money against interest. People engaged in trade went to live in communities and hoped to strengthen their settlements. They needed their own system of law, their own city charter, so that trade and commerce could continue according to modern rules of law. A wave of cities was founded all over Europe. The rulers saw the benefit of this development. Such settlements were important for peace and order in the land, and if the rulers ensured this, the cities would be able – and prepared – to pay taxes. Amsterdam was granted its charter in 1306. It was one of the newest cities in the Netherlands, ranked fifth, after Dordrecht, Haarlem, Delft and Leiden.

The First Church

Amsterdam developed rapidly. The first church, the nucleus of what is now the Oude Kerk (Old Church), was built around 1300. The soil was more solid there than in the rest of the settlement. In the marshy VEENGROND of Holland there are deep layers of sand which rise to the surface in certain places. That was the case here. Later, when the need arose for more solid, heavier building, the beginnings of HEIEN was developed: long tree-trunks or poles ('heipalen') were driven into the ground until they stuck into the layer of sand.

In 1334 Amsterdam became a parish with Saint Nicholas as its patron saint. The Kerkstraat ran beside the church and on the other side of the Amstel was the Windmolenstraat. Between these was the Dam with its adjoining square, the Plaetse. The city even experienced its own 'miracle', the Miracle of Amsterdam, which occurred in 1345. A dying man was administered the Eucharist by a priest. At this the dying man vomited. A woman threw his vomit into the fire, however, what miracle, the host, which had been partly vomited, did not burn. The woman kept the host, but it behaved restlessly. The clergy were informed and the host was taken to the Oude Kerk in solemn procession. A new chapel, the Heilige Stede, was built on the place the miracle had occurred, and in another fire the host was again spared, at which the miracle gained still greater prestige. This place continued to be the scene of miraculous cures.

The city council of Amsterdam consisted of a 'vroedschap' (city council) and four mayors. In 1400 Amsterdam obtained the privilege of naming it's mayors without the permission of the sovereign. Neither did the 'vroedschap' have a say: the mayors ruled the city and named a successor themselves if and when the occasion arose. Nine 'schepenen' (alderman) were the jury and judge of the city, and only when they sentenced someone to death did they need permission form the mayor. This system was undemocratic, indeed, it was a prime example of an olicharchy. However, it was maintained until 1795.

'Mother Commerce'

Because transferring cargo across the Dam was immensely time-consuming, locks were installed. These locks are first mentioned in 1347. There is also mention of a sheriff (or portreeve) of the Dam-sluis (lock). He was charged with maintaining order at and around the locks. In effect the locks formed a tunnel, or a broad bridge. The mast of a ship had to be lowered first before the it could pass through. To this day a stone bridge in Amsterdam is known as a 'sluis'. The locks were originally owned by the water board but gradually the city took over first their management and then the ownership.

The economic flourishing of Amsterdam was based on beer and herring. As early as 1323 Amsterdam was given the exclusive right to import beer from Hamburg. In order to protect native beer brewers, an import duty, which had to be paid in Amsterdam, was imposed. Beer was the universal people's drink in a time without a sewage system. Herring was abundantly available and was an essential element of the people's diet.

From the very beginning the Baltic trade was the most important trade sector, the 'mother of all commerce' for Amsterdam. Herring were caught on the south coast of Sweden and basic necessities of life such as wood (building material) and grain, together with iron ore and valuable furs, were imported from the Balkan countries. However, the Baltic Sea region was controlled by the Hanseatic League, a union of cities stretching along the North Sea and Baltic Sea up to the Gulf of Finland and which had Lübeck as its prestigious centre. Amsterdam, the newcomer in the Baltic trade, sailed through the Oresund, by-passed Lübeck, and came into conflict with vested interests in the Baltic region. A fleet was fitted out and there was a minor war and a great deal of negotiation. In 1441 Amsterdam won the dispute. Free passage through the Oresund would have the highest priority in Amsterdam politics for another two-and-a-half centuries. In about 1400 the mating season of the herring moved to the North Sea and it was around this time that fishermen discovered how to gut these fish. This method entailed the removal of the intestines through the gills immediately after they had been caught, so they did not rot so quickly. Fishermen could now remain at sea for longer periods of time, catch more fish, and subsequently make more profit.

Baltic trade was supplemented by trade with the Mediterranean Sea region from where they got subtropical fruits and the indispensable salt. Amsterdam was the staple market for goods from both quarters.

(p. 16)
The Miracle of Amsterdam: the host that would not burn. Procession-flag, the fireproof host is taken out of the fire. Unknown. (AHM)

Hendrick Cornelisz. Vroom's Dutch three-master advancing the Sont at Fort Kronberg (1614). (Gemalde-gallery Berlin)

Unity and Division 1400–1578

Chapter 2

Philips the Good (1396–1467), Duke of Burgundy, Count of Holland, Zeeland and Henegouwen.
Stedelijke Musea Brugge

(p. 20)
Detail from Albert Cuyp, a VOC merchant and his wife.
RMA

In 1400 the community on the Amstel, which had been the stake in the fierce struggle between the mini-states of Holland and Utrecht, became part of the extensive kingdom of Philip the Good of the House of Burgundy. He wished to unite the many regions of the Netherlands through a combination of the right of succession and conquest. The parties in the struggle called themselves the 'Hoeksen' and the 'Kabeljauwen'. Philip's supporters were largely Kabeljauwen, the party of the burgeoning cities. Amsterdam was one of these. They stood for a strong central authority and political unity. Philip's opponents, the Hoeksen, were under the command of Jacoba van Beieren, Philip the Good's niece. In the main they represented the fragmented feudal past. Philip won the struggle and made peace with Jacoba, 'the unhappy countess', known as the Reconciliation of Delft in 1428. Philip actively supported Amsterdam in the conflict with the Hanseatic League.

After the death of Philip the Good in 1467 the conflict continued to proliferate under his son Charles the Bold and Charles' daughter Mary the Rich, who was married to the Habsburg Maximilian of Austria. The sovereign's objective remained the same – the unification of all the regions of the Netherlands. Gelre held out longest against this policy of unification. Amsterdam took part in the Kabeljauw campaigns and at various times was threatened by the 'Gelderse' troops, led by Maarten van Rossum. In 1489, when the sovereign Maximiliaan , who was predestined to become the future Emperor of Germany, was in big trouble, Amsterdam helped him with a loan of no less than 10.000 pounds. As a token of his appreciation he granted Amsterdam the right to add his crown to the city's coat of arms. Over the years, Amsterdam turned this into an emperor's crown. Such a distinction made a deep impression throughout Europe and had a favourable effect on trade and commerce.

The political unity of all the Netherlands – roughly the present-day

Benelux region – would only actually come about in 1543 under Charles V, the grandson of Maximilian and the great-great grandson of Philip the Good. The Habsburgian Emperor Charles V, the last emperor to have been crowned by the pope, ruled over the European countries Spain and Germany. He was in constant conflict with the Turks on the Mediterranean Sea and because he also ruled the South American colonies of Spain people said of him that in his empire 'the sun never set'. But in al this political turmoil he held steadfast to the goal set out by his ancestors with a view to the Netherlands. This surely says something about the meaning and wealth of these provinces.

The heart of the Netherlands lay in Brussels. How did the 16th century inhabitant look towards this? Do we hear any opinions in Amsterdam, or even pride over having achieved the unity of 1543, which was eternally confirmed three years later in the so-called 'Pragmatic Sanction'? Hardly. One could compare this to the slow expansion of the European Union of our time. The governing elite got used to it quickly. The governors of the cities travelled to congresses, the new each other well. However, the people couldn't care less.

Amsterdam, peaceful after the endless disputes of the Middle Ages, lay on the periphery. It was a breeding ground for the tempestuous growth which was already within reach. It had it's privileges, its confirmed regents and its emperors crown. In 1555 when Charles V abdicated, his empire was divided. Germany and Austria went to his son Ferdinand, Spain and the Netherlands went to his son Phillip II.

The Baltic trade remained the 'mother of commerce'. Amsterdam imported salt – which, among other things, was needed for the herring-trade – from France and Portugal. It was a staples market, where goods from north and south were stored, refined and processed. There was a chain reaction of progress. Industry, technique and science, cartography, printing, banking and insurance businesses all came about to accompany the world trade. The arts flourished, for those who made money wanted to show off their wealth. There was plenty of talent about and it flowed into the city from all quarters. In 1408 Amsterdam obtained a second parish. Willem Eggert, Lord of Purmerend, gave up his orchard for the construction of the St. Catherina, or Nieuwe Kerk (New Church). His memory is honoured by the name of the street that runs behind this church.

Cornelis Anthonisz.

The city of the mid-fourteenth century that we are speaking about is clearly described in a document dating from 1342. It had expanded upstream along the Amstel to the Grimburgwal and the Spui and was further bordered by the IJ, the Oudezijds Voorburgwal and the Nieuwezijds Voorburgwal. Nowadays, these expansions seem trivial, but it is important to realise the vast impact this had for everyday life at that time. Several thousands of people lived there without sanitation or a collection service for rubbish. So what did they do with their rubbish? They threw it into the canal, which was anything but salubrious. The stench lay like a blanket over the city.

Fortunately enough Cornelis Anthonisz. portrayed the city in its Middle Ages compactness. Anthonisz. was a versatile artist, painter, engraver and cartographer. He made his bird's-eye view of Amsterdam in 1538; the woodcut he prepared from the painting dates from 1544. This work is an unparalleled achievement. It is difficult to comprehend how the artist could imagine being at such a high vantage point. At the same time it is a very beautiful work of art.

Dam Square, detail from Cornelis Anthonisz., birds-eye view of Amsterdam around 1538. (AHM)

Cornelis Anthonisz., around 1500–1561. Birds-eye view of Amsterdam around 1538. (AHM)

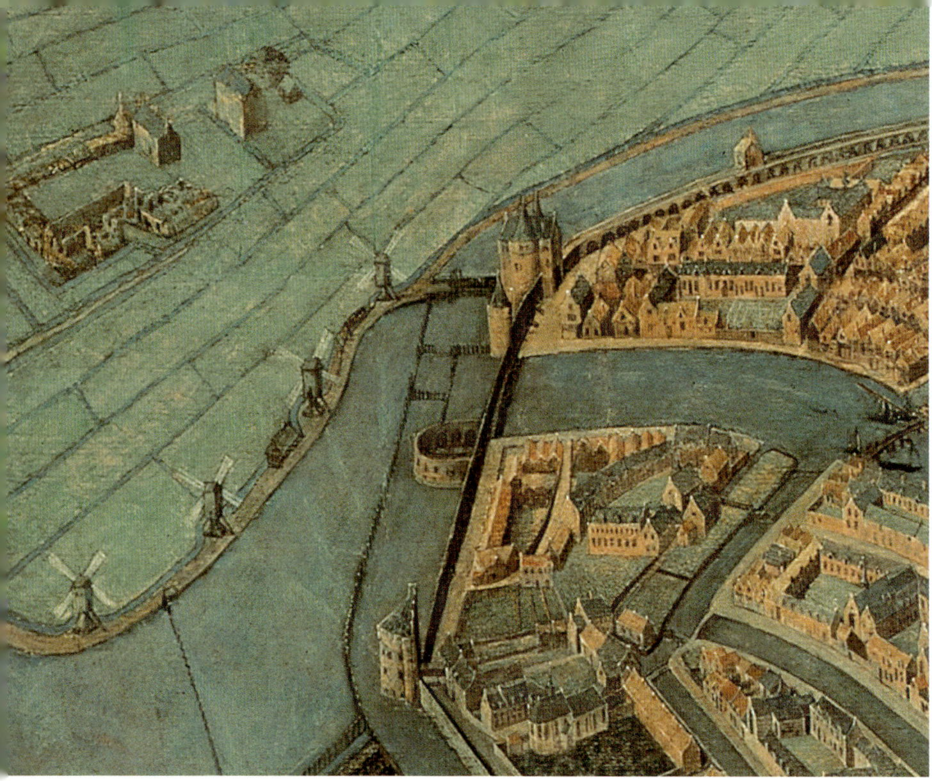

The Regulierspoort, now the Munttoren, detail from Cornelis Anthonisz., birds-eye view of Amsterdam around 1538. (AHM)

We are now speaking of a city with an estimated 30,000 inhabitants. The heart of this city, which still survives today, was then complete and details of it can still be recognised. Upstream the city had expanded to the Munt, where there was a majestic double bend in the Amstel. At the bend, two famous strongpoints, can be seen on the map; the tower with the revealing name 'Swycht Utrecht' (Yield Utrecht) and the Rondeel. In present-day terms, going along with the current, the situation is as follows: coming from the Carré, past the Stopera, we reach the Doelen Hotel and the Hotel de L'Europe, which have replaced the Swycht Utrecht and the Rondeel. The city of 1538 was bordered on the west side by the Singel, which at the Munt became, as it still does, the Binnen-Amstel. From there onwards it continued into the Kloveniersburgwal. On the Nieuwmarkt stood the Sint Antoniespoort – now the Waag -, which you had to pass through to enter the city. The city gate was a link in the original seawall. The Geldersekade then led to the IJ. Storm defences closed off the IJ across the whole breadth of the city.

Outside these borders were areas of racks or 'ramen' (windows) used by the textile industry to dry its dyed cloth. We still have a 'Verversstraat' (Dyers' Street) and the word 'raam' appears in the street names in five different places. The 'lijnbanen' (rope walks) where rope was manufactured were also originally outside the city walls. However, in the industrial areas outside the city houses were also built for newcomers, adventurers and entrepreneurs. This development could be witnessed especially on the east side of the town, where the Lastage (now called the Nieuwmarkt district) was a bustling industrial area with shipyards, ropewalks, smithies and other relevant industries. The Geldersen, however, put the Lastage to the torch on various occasions. This was the reason the city government built the Montelbaanstoren (tower) at its eastern point as a defensive bastion. (The decorative pinnacle by Hendrik de Keyser is of a later date). In around 1600, at the insistence of its inhabitants, the city brought the Lastage and the artificial islands further to the east, containing shipbuilding and other industries, within the boundaries of the city.

We see that on the Dam-locks there was a fish market and that next to it there was still room for two rows of houses. On the Plaetse stood a Gothic town hall, which was rebuilt after the great city fire of 1421. However, the Plaetse was much smaller than the present-day Dam. The town hall was more to the fore than the present-day palace, and stood in alignment with the Kalverstraat and the Nieuwendijk. Furthermore, between the town hall and the Nieuwe Kerk there was still room for a street, seven plots, another street, and another five plots. A striking feature is the presence of so many enclosed green areas in this still small city. These were the many monasteries and convents with their gardens, some of which are still remembered in street names such as Bethaniënstraat and Gebed zonder end. The structure of these monasteries can still be recognised in the Begijnehof, in both inner courtyards of the old

The Schreierstoren, detail from Cornelis Anthonisz., birds-eye view of Amsterdam around 1538. (AHM)

St. Anthonispoort, now the Waag, detail from Cornelis Anthonisz., birds-eye view of Amsterdam around 1538. (AHM)

town hall on Oudezijds Voorburgwal, now The Grand hotel, and in the terrain of the Binnengasthuis, once the site of two convents, the 'Oude Nonnen' and the 'Nieuwe Nonnen'.

Cornelis Anthonisz. painting shows three bridges across the Damrak. The centre element of these bridges could be opened so that seagoing ships could sail up to the Dam without striking their masts.

In 1565, after Cornelis Anthonisz., the Waag (weigh house), isolated on the Dam, was built. In 1599 the fish market was housed on the original Dam, in a building with a covered market, together known as the 'Huis onder 't Zeil' (House under the Sail). Since 1956 the National Monument has stood at this spot.

Reformation

Luther's appearance in 1517 precipitated Europe into a long series of religious wars. In 1535 Amsterdam was startled by the Anabaptist insurrection. The Anabaptists were a sect who believed that in the name of Christian equality, social differences must also disappear. To express their conviction they ran in honest nakedness through the streets. Forty men and women even managed to occupy the town hall. The ringleaders were quickly arrested and punished mercilessly. Social insurgency was not tolerated. The sentence read: "The breast to be cut open while still living; the heart pulled out and thrown into the face, after which they are to be beheaded and quartered." The heads were then mounted on stakes at the city gates and the remains of the bodies hung up outside the city. The city government, which had allowed matters to reach so far, was replaced by a stronger regime. For a long time Amsterdam would remain averse to any religious reformation whatsoever.

The religious struggle would mean the end of the unity of all the Netherlands which Charles V had established with such great efforts. Charles' son, Philip II, had become king of Spain through right of succession. People felt that Charles V, who was born in Ghent, belonged to this country – the emperor spoke a little Flemish. However, his son Philip retreated to the Escorial and from there hoped to stamp out the

Execution of the The Anabaptists on the Dam in 1535. Coloured engraving by Jan van Gensel. (GAA)

reformation in the Netherlands. In 1525, Jan de Bakker, a parish priest of Woerden, who had switched to the reformation, was the first to die at the stake as a heretic.

Was there a feeling of nationality in the Netherlands? In any event, all the regions in the Netherlands had a long tradition of merging. Despite all the party disputes the pinnacle of that process was reached in 1543. For centuries a small group of noble families, to which the Nassau family belonged, had occupied high administrative positions; cities had their trading contacts and they had been at state meetings. There was a powerful body which enjoyed privileges and acquired rights, and there was already a Dutch-German language with its own literature. These combined factors were sufficient enough to be able to

Adriaan Key, William of Orange. (RMA)

speak of a 'fatherland', as the word was used in the Wilhelmus (the Dutch national anthem), which was written in 1568. Fatherland? This concept was to be further defined, for the sovereign of the Netherlands lived far away in Spain and was represented here by governors, later by one governor.

The Dutch Revolt 1568–1648

The Netherlands rose against the Spanish sovereign and his Spanish troops. They had had enough of the religious persecutions and wanted to retain their old freedoms. Willem van Nassau, who by right of success was soon to become Prince of the Principality of Orange, was a member of the high governing nobility. He was a member of the Council of State and Stadhouder (viceroy) – the king's deputy – of Holland, Zeeland and Utrecht. He was the leader of the insurrection, which began in 1568. In 1572 almost every city in Holland and Zeeland, except Amsterdam and Middelburg, chose the Prince's side. The Spanish troops struck back. Mechelen, Zutphen and Naarden were destroyed and with Amsterdam as their base the Spanish were able to besiege

Haarlem. Haarlem held out for seven months in the winter of 1572–1573. The city could not be starved into submission because the insurgents, who called themselves 'geuzen' (beggars), continued to provide the city of food via the Haarlemmermeer. But Amsterdam chose the Spanish side. Unfortunately a Spanish fleet from Amsterdam managed to reach the Haarlemmermeer across the Schinkel and defeated the Geuzen fleet. Hunger then forced Haarlem to surrender. Many, among which the flower of Dutch knighthood, were beheaded by the Spaniards. Waal mercenaries, who had once sworn an oath never again to fight against the Spanish, were tied back to back in pairs and thrown into the Spaarne to drown. The Spanish now controlled a line between Amsterdam and Haarlem; the northern quarter was isolated, the insurgency appeared to be over. But in that same year – 1573 – in the watery North Holland, Spain, a world power, experienced its own Vietnam. The insurgents struck back at the Spanish troops near Alkmaar and the Geuzen fleet defeated Amsterdam, Spain's allies, in the Zuiderzee near Hoorn.

The Alteration

What followed was a small-scale civil war. In 1567 the Geuzen-leader Herman Helling attacked Amsterdam which was rebuked. After this the Geuzen took the city under siege. On Februari 8 1578 Amsterdam drew political conclusions from the military situation and signed the treaty of 'satisfaction' or 'reconciliation' with the prince of Orange and the Provinces of Holland. A few months later Protestants and members of the prince's party replaced the city government, a process which was termed the 'Alteration' or 'change'. The old city government and the Roman Catholic clergy were set afloat on the Zuiderzee from the IJ on two barges and landed outside the city on the Diermerzeedijk. This was neither very nice or very friendly, but at least we can say that no blood was spilt. The Oude Kerk (or St. Nicolaaskerk) and the Nieuwe Kerk were stripped of their Roman Catholic character and from then on were used for reformed worship.

The rulers, however, were tolerant and averse to dogmatism. There were many religiously mixed marriages in the wealthiest circles. A blind eye was turned to Catholic worship in convents. For example, in 1641 the Franciscans established a secret church behind the facades of the merchants Mozes and Aäron in the Jewish quarter, which officially was named after St. Antonius of Padua, but which was generally known as the Moses and Aäron church. (the present-day church building came into service in 1861). In 1661 the Ons' Lieve Heer op Solder (Our Lord in the Attic) church was established in a narrow canal house in which a number of floors were broken out. Here Amsterdam's patron saint, St. Nicholas, was worshipped. (After 1887, when the new church of St. Nicholas was completed, Ons' Lieve Heer op Solder was retained as a museum). The Mennonites had their secret place of worship on the

Singel near the Koningsplein (next to the present-day church De Krijtberg). The Lutherans were able to openly build their circular church on the Singel, and this came into use in 1671. This is now the Sonesta Congress Centre.

Through the 'satisfaction' and 'alteration' the isolation of Amsterdam came to an end and the city was able to continue its turbulent growth.

The Union of Utrecht

One of the most infamous attempts to conquer Amsterdam was Colonel Helling's attack on the city in 1577. During this attack four platoons managed to enter the city, but they were quickly driven out. (AHM)

Once again Amsterdam became part of another group of states. In 1579 the Netherlands definitively split up into the Union of Atrecht and the Union of Utrecht. The Union of Atrecht made peace with Spain. The Union of Utrecht continued its resistance under the leadership of the Prince of Oranje. After a few changes in alliances, the Union of Utrecht now consisted of seven members: Holland, Zeeland, Utrecht, Gelre, the Oversticht, Friesland and Groningen (Drenthe was too poor to be a full member). The Union was a loose federation, governed by the States General, the representatives of the provincial nobility and bourgeoisie. They met, as tradition had it, in The Hague. Formally the King of Spain was the ultimate ruler; William of Orange was his viceroy, or represen-

tative, and derived his authority from this. In 1580 the Prince visited Amsterdam, the city that had chosen his side in 1578. He received a warm reception, but it soon proved that love for him did not run very deep.

After the Union of Utrecht in 1581 had renounced the King of Spain, a new state appeared on the European stage – the Republic of the Seven United Netherlands (although it was still not generally recognised). The question now arose as to whom should become the highest authority in the land. Prince William of Orange appeared to be the obvious person, but when in December 1583 the States of Holland wanted to offer him the count's power it was inhibited from doing so due to Amsterdam's resistance. Couldn't the States General simply proclaim it? In 1584, before agreement was reached, the Prince was murdered at his house in Delft. The States General now assumed the highest authority. They were the guardians of the freedoms and the tolerance based on privileges handed down from the Middle Ages. The court of Orange moved from Delft to The Hague. In 1585 Prince Maurits, the son of Prince Willem, was appointed viceroy, although there was no longer a king in which name he could be deputy. This viceroy was Captain-General of the entire Union. Formally, Maurits and his successors were only civil servants in the service of the States, but their function was hereditary. The viceroy derived his authority from his noble descent and his actual power from his military function. It was an uncomfortable coexistence of republican privileges and rights of succession.

While other countries in Europe were developing towards centralisation and government by a single head of state, the Union of Utrecht remained a medieval remain, a hobnob of rights and privileges. An old-fashioned system? Certainly, but at the same time the Union was the defender of a principle that would one day become progressive once more. When the Americans were preparing their constitution at the end of the 18th century they looked upon the Republic with awe. For the Americans at that time it was an inspiring example of civil freedom made possible by the principle of decentralised power. The Republic was not a democracy. Privileges were for the rich. The lower classes had

Profile of Amsterdam, seen from the IJ, by Pieter van der Keere (1618). The Latin text underneath the painting describes the city and its history. Thirty-five buildings are described.

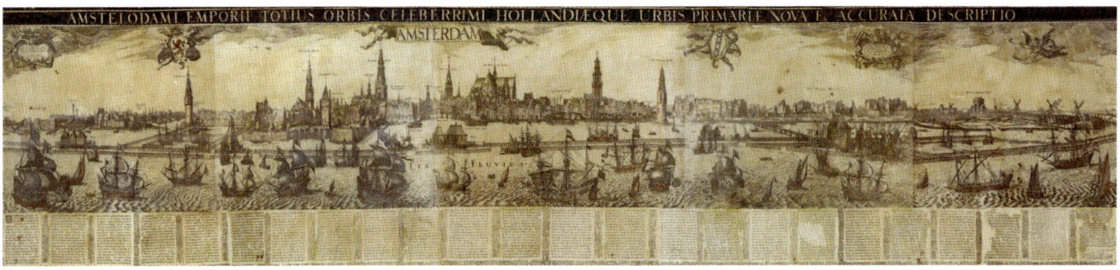

ra Virgini &
hodie novum
pulchritudine
opæ Basilicas
. Præterhæc
ea illud quod
quidem hope-
nihilominus
ta factum, ut
ustrarum præ-
& alia. Sed in-
mstelodamensis
n Zuyder Kerc-
m non in Or-
a, sed in Au-
gantissimis &
s fenestris vi-
o tenore ac si-

mili sibi per omnia lapide (sarcophagos
appellant) constratum est. Vnde & pluri-
mum reliquæ totius operis symmetriæ
decoris ac venustatis accedit: ut etiam a
turri cujus pulchritudine hæc ædes specta-
bilis est. Quid de Xenodocheo, Procho-
dochijs, & Orphanotrophio dicam? Quid
de Nosodochio Leprosorum, Aula divi
Georgij, Gyrgato seu mẽte captorum do-
mo? Quid de Curia, Libra, Sagittariorum
hortis, Aula principis, & Societatis Indi-
canæ domo & similibus? Vtroque in urbis
latere, novo nimirum & veteri, ludus se-
orsum literarius est, Ecclesiæ & Reipubli-
cæ seminarium, & cuique, præter inferio-
res moderatores, Rector Prorectorq; con-
stitutis, additis in usum eorum reliquo-
rumque docentium, pro cujusq; conditio-

ne & modo stipendijs. Sed inter omnia
præclara ædificia urbis primi censendum
[illegible] Gerontomium, visendum sane opus.
In meditullio duplex est sepimẽtum sive
hortus: quorum alter floribus & arbore-
tis areolisq; non inconcinne distinguitur.
Alter viridario ornatur, quod gramine
solummodo constitum, aspectum vel hoc
ipso delectat. Vtriumque a lateribus & a
fronte quoq; porticus & laquearia sunt,
ambulacri vicem præbentia: Et proxime
sub his conclavia virorum mulierumque,
separatim ac ordino disposita, lectisque
alia supellectile decenter exornata. In-
terstitium quod est intra viridarium &
hortum, recto in ipsum ædificium ac lato
aditu ducit, haud levibus impẽsis nec ine-
leganter fabrefactum: Præter enim atria

magnificia nitentiaque, cœnacula sunt bi-
na, quorum alterum fœminis, maribus
alterum patet; culina his addita: & omnia
eum in modum aptata cõcinnataque, ut
nõ pauperum sed Principis palatium ap-
paratumque dicamus. Quid de Ergaste-
rijs dicam? Bina hæc dunt, alterum Mari-
um, feminarum alterum. In priore deti-
nentur Mendici, Nequam, & perditi, om-
nes conclusi, nonnulli etiam compedibus
vincti, ita tamen ut operi vacare manusq;
exercere libere queant. Alij enim aut acá-
thinum lignum (Brasilianum vulgo) in
scobem tenuissimam disterere ac tyroc-
nesti comminuere, aut pãnos deniq; bom-
basios contexere, aliaque agere atque ela-
borare coguntur, prout vel ingenium vel
artus cujusque ac robur suadere videtur.

Dominicis feriatisq; diebus adesse tener
tur cuncti in loco quam Scholam voca
Hic in sacris nonnihil prælegitur, præse
tim si quid ad mores & vitæ frugem fa
Nonnulli etiam in primis literarum ele
mentis legendo scribẽdoque exercentu
Hoc autem loco om[illegible]tẽdum neutiqua
videtur de hujus loci miraculis. Nimi
varios mendicos, ulcera ostentantes
[illegible] vitia, involucris obscœnis ac fa-
cijs tecta, corporisque claudicationes, al
aque ejusmodi visu fœda: itemq; mut
aliquot & Lunaticos ac demoniacos hu
introductos, post aliquot temporis spa
um fascijs & involucris, bacillisq; quibu
innitebantur, alijsque similibus, que fi
cum populo faciebãt, abjectis, agiles m
detecta scena, ad opus processisse omne

Detail from Pieter van der Keere's Profile of Amsterdam, seen from the IJ (1618). (GAA)

The VOC's flute ship De Hoop around 1718. Drawing in water colour, presumably by J. Houck. (NSA)

no voice, or if they had, it was the power of the word preached by orthodox ministers every Sunday from the pulpit.

Once again Amsterdam lay outside the centre of power. It was able to exercise influence, however, because influence in the Republic was proportional to the financial contribution paid by a province or a city. Because of this Holland carried weight in the Union and Amsterdam carried weight in Holland. A burgomaster of Amsterdam could rightly be termed a 'citizen king'.

To the Indies

At the end of the fifteenth century navigators in the service of Portugal and Spain undertook the great voyages of discovery – everyone knows about the voyages to America by Christopher Columbus (1492) and to the Indies by Vasco da Gama (1498). Holland and Zeeland, which around 1440 had so rapidly defeated the Hanseatic League, did not make these voyages until one hundred years later.

At first it was completely unnecessary to risk voyaging to the Indies. The Netherlands bought colonial goods in Lisbon and traded them on; they invested less than the Portuguese, and made more profit. But when the Spanish king annexed Portugal in 1580, Lisbon became dangerous for Dutch ships. The Northern Dutchmen were now compelled to seek the sea passage to the Indies themselves. They were helped in this by the fact that after 1585, when Antwerp fell into the hands of the

Spanish, many Southern Dutch merchants came to Amsterdam. Although they were forced to leave their material wealth behind, they brought with them the priceless wealth of their knowledge and expertise. Among them were Portuguese Jews who had fled to Antwerp from Portugal. A great additional advantage for Holland and Zeeland, and for Amsterdam in particular, was the closing of the Schelde, which crippled Antwerp. Amsterdam benefited greatly. This might not be particularly sporting, but it was simply how it was. In a few years time Amsterdam made the leap forward, which led to the unique flourishing of the Golden Age. In 1595 the 'First Voyage' left Amsterdam for the Indies. Cornelis de Houtman, who returned two years later but made no profit, commanded the fleet. The second fleet, under the command of Jacob Cornelisz. van Neck, sailed in 1598. It returned a year later with a cargo that yielded 400% profit.

Around 1600, and for a long time afterwards, the introduction of the flute ship gave the Hollanders, especially the citizens of Amsterdam, an advantage over their competitors. This type of ship was created at the end of the sixteenth century in Hoorn. Prof. A. Wegener Sleeswyk has called it a revolutionary design. Although types of ship at this time were not standardised, the flute nonetheless had a number of fixed characteristics. It was a slim three-master with a flat counter (stern). The hull curved steeply inwards, which gave the flute a large cargo capacity, but because the freeboards curved inwards so strongly the deck surface was small compared to the rounded hull. This was important because the Oresund toll was calculated on the surface area of the deck.

In proportion to its breadth, the flute was longer than was usual for ships – such as the kogge – at that time, which found it very difficult to sail against the wind. Because the flute was longer and slimmer it was able to sail quite close to the wind. It was also lighter in build and needed fewer crewmembers. A kind of industrial revolution was going on in Noord-Holland. In 1594 Cornelisz Cornelisz of Uitgeest had constructed the first saw-mill. The aim was to replace strenuous hand-labour by mechanical labour. The steam-engine hadn't been invented yet, but wind-power temporarily took its place. Shipbuilding was made cheaper by the invention of the saw-mill. Once again this gave the Netherlands a head start over its foreign competitors, just as the use of wind for reclaiming the great lakes of Noord-Holland would do a few years later.

The VOC

Throughout the whole of Holland and Zeeland companies were set up and fleets fitted out to make the voyage to the East Indies. The States General gave Johan van Oldenbarnevelt, state attorney of Holland, the task of combining all these initiatives. Thanks to his exceptional diplo-

The return to Amsterdam of the second expedition to the East. Indies, 1599
RMA

matic skills Oldenbarnevelt succeeded in doing this. The Dutch East India Company (VOC), the first public limited company in the world, came into being in 1602. The start-up capital for the VOC was a meagre 6.5 million guilders, 3.5 million of which was contributed by Amsterdam, more than half. Seventeen governors administered the VOC, eight of whom were named by Amsterdam – not quite half, because people were afraid of Amsterdam domination.

The founding of the VOC touched the entire population of Amsterdam. Only 84 of the more than one thousand shareholders were really large investors (10,000 guilders or more). In contrast, on the list of subscribers were 466 typical small investors, who subscribed less than 1000 guilders. They formed two fifths of the total number. They were the small, self-employed craftsmen of the time – a brief look at these people will enable us to better understand the industrious people of Amsterdam. To mention just a few from a long list: 'boxs'-maker (boxs were leather trousers), glove maker, cloak maker, sock maker, lantern maker, spoon maker, sugar refiner, wagoner, soap boiler, and silk weaver. These people had had some schooling and could sign their names.

Subscriptions were also taken out by waged labourers, such as weighing-house porters, linen packers, a seamstress, a midwife and seven domestic servants, including Grietgen Dirckxdochter, 'Burgomaster Boom's maid' (for 60 guilders); Trijntgen Pickers, 'living in the house of Martijn Jans, convoy master (for 60 guilders); Claessien Claes, 'knitter'; and Giert Jans, maidservant, for each of whom Renier Pauw subscribed 100 guilders. Most of them could not write and signed with a cross. A small share of 60 to 100 guilders was nonetheless a large part of their savings. Real enthusiasm had seized the city.

In 1621 the West India Company (WIC) was founded. This company was responsible for the founding of New Amsterdam. Under the 1667 Treaty of Breda, however, the Dutch ceded this city to Britain in exchange for Surinam. New Amsterdam became New York.

Albert Cuyp, a VOC merchant and his wife. On the background we can see the return fleet at the dock of the Batavia. (RMA)

Jewish 'Amsterdammers'

Amongst the many foreigners this great city attracted the Jews held a particular place in its history. During the Diaspora after the destruction of the temple in 70 AD, the Jews had dispersed in two directions from the Mediterranean Sea – via Spain and via Russia. The Jews from Spain and Portugal were known as the Sephardic Jews, those from Poland and Germany as the Ashkenazy Jews. These two streams came together in Amsterdam. For them Amsterdam was the 'city of cities' – Great Mokum. The first place they established themselves was on the terrain at the bend in the Amstel which was regularly flooded and called 'Vloeienburg' or 'Vloônburg' (one meaning of 'vloeien' in Dutch is to 'flood'). It's name was derived from the fact that it flooded regularly. However, at the end of the 16th century it just been drained and reclaimed.

The business and commercial elite was tolerant here. The Jews enjoyed great freedom, but they had no access to the guilds – the tightly knit craft and commercial organisations. The diamond processing industry had no guild and could therefore become a Jewish business branch. But the Jews were always in danger. In times of need it was not unknown for strongly Calvinistic ministers to incite the people to plunder the Jewish quarter. The regents could do little more than send messengers to the Jewish quarter with a warning.

The Jewish quarter expanded from Vloônburg towards the sea dike, the present-day Jodenbreestraat and Sint Antoniesbreestraat, and still further to the eastern islands. But there was no question of a ghetto; the proportion of Jews to non-Jews was roughly fifty-fifty. One example is Rembrandt, who wasn't Jewish, but lived in the heart of the Jewish quarter in the large house at Jodenbreestraat 4, which is now a museum, from 1639 to 1660. Towards the end of the 17th century the Portuguese and the Dutch synagogues were built on what is now the Jonas Daniël Meyerplein.

Van Everdingen, the glue manufacturer at the Lange Blekerspad, with Amsterdam's silhouette on the horizon, around 1620. (GAA)

Vlooienburg, map by Floris van Berckenrode (1625). This land, where the Stopera now stands, had only shortly before 1600 been reclaimed. . This was were the Jewish neighbourhood started. The circle indicates the diggings that have been made. They found chicken bones in a cesspit, whilst the neighbours cesspit only contained pig bones. This was evidence to the fact that Jews and non-Jews lived next to each other.

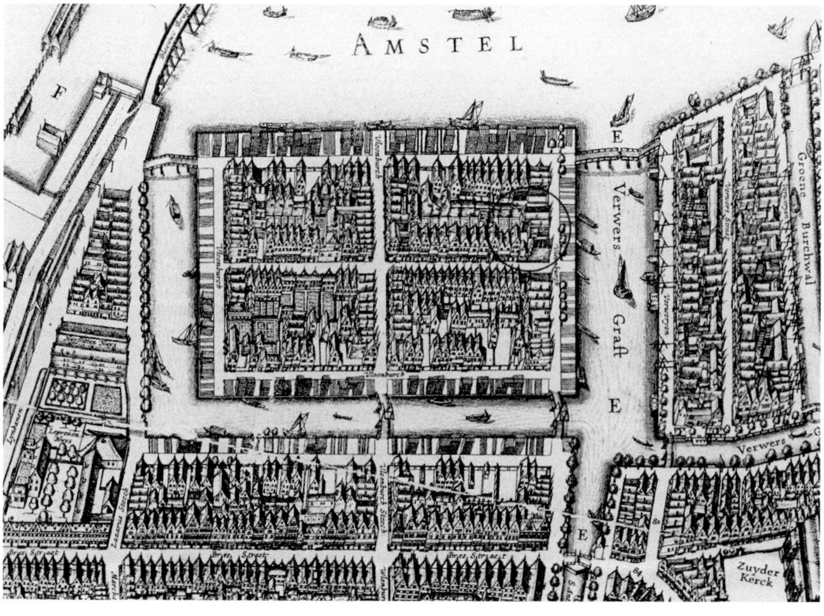

Three synagogues. ?-century etching by Abraham Rademaker. To the left the Portugese-Israeli synagogue (1675). On the forefront, to the right, the High-German synagogue (1670) and, to the right of that the New synagogue with its dome (1752). (GAA)

The Waag on the Dam, which was demolished in 1808. Drawing by P.V. la Fargue, around 1760. (GAA).

The Golden Age 1600–1700

Chapter 3

The seventeenth century was an age of glory for the Netherlands in general and for Amsterdam in particular. A passion for enterprise, wealth, power, tolerance and culture went hand in hand. Amsterdam was rich. One of the wonders of the Golden Age is the fact that after the uprooting of the social elite in the early years of the Insurrection against Spain a new group of leaders managed to emerged very quickly. These leaders' grandparents had been illiterate farmers, and yet they were incredibly successful in world trade and world politics. Amsterdam was rich. The Amsterdam 'Wisselbank', founded by the city government in 1609, was established in the town hall. This Wisselbank brought a giro payment system into being.

Only a rough estimate of the population of Amsterdam can be given – in around 1600: 40,000; in 1610: 50,000; in 1622: 105,000; in 1662: 210,000; and in 1670: 200,000. A century later, in 1795, a census indicated that this number had only grown by a scanty 21,000 to 221,000. From these figures it appears that there was a tumultuous growth at the beginning of the Golden Age, a growth that did not continue after 1670. In 1663 and 1664 our country was struck by a plague, the last and worst of a series of plagues that had ravaged Europe since the Black Death of 1348. According to reports of the time some 34,000 people died of the plague in Amsterdam. Even if this total is exaggerated, as claims the Amsterdam historian H. Brugmans, the death toll was still a considerable 10% of the total population of 210,000 in 1662.

(p. 46)
Detail from Gerrit Adriaensz. Berkenheyde, the city hall on the Dam in the second half of the seventeenth century. (AHM)

The 'Three Canals-plan'

During the Golden Age Amsterdam greatly expanded when the famous ring of canals, designed by Hendrick Staets (1612), was constructed. The Herengracht, Keizersgracht and Prinsengracht were dug as a threesome commencing from their starting point at Brouwersgracht; and at first they went no further than the Leidsegracht. The land had to be bought from the farmers. Mayor Frans Oetgers is infamous in this respect. He abused his foreknowledge when he bought the land cheap only to sell it to the city at a high price. His college, Mayor C. P. Hooft, accused him of 'eigensoekelijkheid' (self-interest), but this wasn't a crime. After having dug the canals the city depended on people buying a lot to build houses on it. These capital buildings were meant as houses to live in, but at the same time they functioned as warehouses. The canals were in fact an extension to the harbour. The houses were narrow in comparison, whilst they stretched out inwards quite far. The oldest front was the step-roof with stone ornaments. More fanciful was the neck-gable, whereby the step-roof was simplified and brought down to one step. The sharp corner of the neck-gable could be filled up with statues of dolphins or sea-gods. The corner could also be rounded, creating the so-called Dutch gable. Sometimes the front was decorated with pilasters, an ornament strongly resembling Greek pillars. Garlands and

AMSTELODAMI CELEBERRIMI HOLLANDIÆ
Notularum Explicatio
Aemstela fluvius
YA FLVV
PRÆTORI, CONSVLIBVS, SCABINIS,
I. Blaeu

Map of Amsterdam, by Johan Bleau (1649). (Scheepvaartmuseum Amsterdam)

Gerrit Berckheyde (1638–1698), the bend in the Herengracht. Berckheyde left out the trees to give the fine architecture the full prominence it deserves. RMA

festoons together with statues of dolphins and sea-gods could give the front a more distinguished character. Al these narrow houses showed a rich variation. The Amsterdam canal houses, as we know them now, are mostly much taller than those in the old hearts of other cities in the Netherlands. Five stories with a height of about 16 metres are no exception. Towards the end of the Seventeenth century newly built houses were made taller, something which suited the status of metropolis that

Jan van der Heyden, Keizersgracht with the Westerkerk. Drawn around 1660. (GAA)

Amsterdam had. The city government encouraged people to make existing houses taller. It gave the town more air. In this process the old-fashioned step-roofs were modernised to become neck-gables or Dutch gables.

The reformed churches Zuiderkerk, Westerkerk, Oosterkerk and Noorderkerk were built in the first half of the 17th century. Nine towers dominated the silhouette of the city, the houses of which at that time

The Stock Exchange by the city's master builder Hendrick de Keyser. (GAA)

were still low. Five of these remain – those of the Oude Kerk, the Zuiderkerk and Westerkerk, and the non-religious Montelbaanstoren and Munttoren. The tower of the Oudekerk, 1565, was designed by Joost Janz. Beeldsnijder (also known as Bilhamer). Hendrick de Keyser (1565–1621) designed the others. Other famous Amsterdam architects were Adriaan Dortsman (Amstel 216); the brothers Johannes Vingboons (the Cromhout houses, Herengracht 364-370, where the Bible Museum is established), Justus Vingboons (the Trippen house on Kloveniers-burgwal); and Daniël Stalpaert, who completed the town hall and drew the city map of 1658.

There was much charity in the rich town, and the poor, elderly and orphans much needed it. The Old Orphanage (Oude Burgerweeshuis) in the Kalverstraat has been restored and since 1975 it houses the Amsterdams Historisch Museum. The entry gate is decorated with a beautiful relief under which one can read the words of Vondel: 'We grow fast in amount and burden, our second fathers complain, Ay, do not pass under this gate, without helping to carry the burden. Other buildings in the city which remind us of the past charities are the Oudemanhuis-

The gate of the Burgerweeshuis, now the entrance of the Amsterdams Historisch Museum.

The ledger of the Burgerweeshuis, the register in which the children were inscribed. Dates from around 1630. (GAA)

poort and the Maagdenhuis, both now owned by the university. Also, the Oudezijds Huiszitten Huis for the elderly, in which the Academie voor Bouwkunst is now situated. There were numerous courtyards and gardens for the elderly, whose inhabitants were solely dependant on charity. Of those there are still a few left.

The economic expansion was unimaginable. Lodewijk de Geer and his brother-in-law Elias Trip were the biggest arms manufacturers in Europe. Lodewijk de Geer established iron foundries and arms factories in Sweden. The chimneys of the Trippen house represented gun barrels.

Amsterdam invested in the reclamation of the large lakes in North Holland; first the Beemster in 1609, followed by the Purmer, the Schermer and the Wormer. Jan Adriaensz. Leeghwater, a miller in De Rijp, led these huge enterprises. The polders provided agricultural land, but earlier on they also provided land for country estates and idyllic spots for the Amsterdam nouveaux riche.

Culture

Culture flourished. The composer and organ player Jan Pietrsz. Sweelinck enjoyed European fame. The brothers Francois and Pierre Hemony from Lotharingen supplied the churches and town hall with clocks. They were the most famous bell-founders of their time. Their workplace was situated on the Molenpad. There were the poets Bredero, P.C: Hooft and Vondel. In 1617 Samuel Coster founded the literary com-

Two copper etchings of father and son Hooft. Left Cornelis Pietersz. Hooft (J. Lamsvelt), and right Pieter Cornelisz. Hooft (R. Perzijn).

panionship the ' Nederduytsche Acadamie', from which the first city theatre came forth. Pieter Cornelisz. Hooft, son of the mayor Cornelis Pieterszoon, wrote ornamental love poetry in the renaissance style, like the dialogue between Galathea and her lover:

Galathea, see the new day is born,
No my love, let us linger,
It is the stars,
No my love, let us linger, it is the moon.

And of spontaneous love poetry:

Will it never be again, with the passing of this moment,
The friendship of your eyes, the lustfulness of your lips?

Bredero with his motto: *'t kan verkeeren'* .(GAA)

Hooft was the bailiff, judge of Muiden. There he played host to his literary friends in what he called the 'Muiderkring'. Anna and Maria Tesselschade, the literary gifted daughters of Roemer Visscher, visited often, as did the learned Vossius and Barlaeus. They took a sailboat to get there.

Rembrandt, born in Leiden in 1606 came to Amsterdam in 1631 and bought the monumental building on the Jodenbreestraat 4, in which the museum the 'Rembrandthuis' is now situated, in 1639. This is where he sold his art and had his apprentices work for him, amongst which were Govert Flinck, Ferdinand Bol, Nicolaas Maes, Samuel van Hoogstraten and Carel Fabritius. In the courtyard there was space to paint the Nachtwacht (1642). In 1660 Rembrandt was having financial troubles, his mortgage weighed heavily on him, and he was subsequently forced to sell the house.

Amsterdam was also home to the painter-inventor Jan van den Heijden, inventor of the fire engine; to the naturalist Jan Swammerdam, to the map printer Johan Blaeu, to the Jewish philosopher Baruch de Spinoza – who, however, was driven out of the city because of his views and subsequently died in The Hague – and to the exiled French philosopher René Descartes. Artus Quellinus made the carvings in the town hall, Rombout Verhulst made De Ruyter's mausoleum in the Nieuwe Kerk. But the true glory of Amsterdam sculpting lay in the anonymous art of the front and gable stones.

Vondel

With his enormous love for the city, his utter devotion to free language; his deep piety, his love of Baroque duplication and working in contrasts; his warm love of people and his grief at the death of his son Constantijn and the death of his daughter Saartje, more than any other artist, the poet Joost van den Vondel epitomises Seventeenth Century

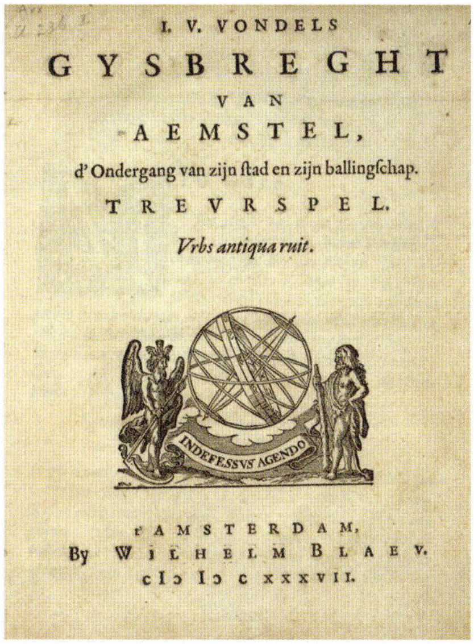

I. V. VONDELS
GYSBREGHT
VAN
AEMSTEL,
d'Ondergang van zijn stad en zijn ballingschap.
TREVRSPEL.
Vrbs antiqua ruit.
INDEFESSVS AGENDO
t'AMSTERDAM,
By WILHELM BLAEV.
cIɔ Iɔ c XXXVII.

Joost van den Vondel. (GAA)

Titlepage of Vondel's Gijsbrecht van Aemstel, 1637.

Amsterdam. Those who know his poem *Op de dood van mijn dochterken* (On the death of my little daughter) can see that the focus in poetry and prose on childhood was not a discovery of the Romantic period, but also existed at this time. People loved their children very much, and, just like us, suffered when one of them died. As far as religion was concerned Vondel was a liberal. In different epigrams he chose for the Arminians or Remonstrants and against Prince Maurits, who had allowed the beheading of Oldebarnevelt, to whom he dedicated his play *Palamedes of de vermoorde onnozelheid* (Palamedes or the murdered innocent). Finally Vondel found comfort and the fulfilment of his visions in his conversion to Roman Catholicism in about 1641. This was a step too far for some of his Remonstrant friends; the Muider circle. P.C. Hooft's very liberal literary society never invited him again. Vondel wrote his play *De Leeuwendalers*, which was successful at that time, in honour of the Treaty of Munster.

In 1632 Amsterdam opened its Athenaeum Illustre, not a university, but nonetheless a prestigious institute of higher education, with Caspar van Baerle and Gerard Vossius as the first professors. The Athanaeum Illustre was established in the Agnietenkapel, the chapel of the former convent of St. Agnes.

Agnietenkapel, where the Atheneum Illustre started.

Peace and a new town hall

In 1648 the Treaty of Munster (known in Europe as the Treaty of Westphalia) was signed. This marked the end of the Netherlands' Eighty Years War and of the Thirty years War in Germany. It was the first conference that encompassed the whole of Europe – only England, at that time torn apart by civil war, was not present.

Our country was free of Spanish claims and independent of the German Empire. Amsterdam was at the pinnacle of its vigour and decided to build a huge town hall, designed by Jacob van Campen. Opposition to the town hall plan came from the strict Presbyterians, led by Mayor William Backer. They had rather honour God by building a high tower to add to the Nieuwe Kerk. I was a fierce debate, which was seemingly won by the Presbyterians. Piles were sunk for the tower and they started building. One can still see the foundations of the tower at the Nieuwezijds Voorburgwal. However, the city-government realised that they could not complete both plans at the same time. In 1652 the old town hall burnt down and in the same year Mayor Backer died. The tower-plan was cancelled

The Plaetse needed to become almost twice as large. An entire row of houses as far as the Nieuwe Kerk was demolished. The first pile was driven in 1648. In 1652 the charming Gothic town hall burned down.

J. A. Beerstraten, the burning of the old city hall in 1652. (AHM)

In 1653 Jacob van der Ulft made a drawing of the Dam, which included a high tower next to the Nieuwe Kerk which had never been built. It stood next to the city hall, which, at that time, had not been completed. (GAA)

The new town hall was rapidly completed and it came into service in 1655. Since then this remarkable building, in classical Baroque style, has dominated the heart of the Netherlands. No imposing outside staircases, no balconies, no impressive entrances, no lively decoration. Only large facade statues, in which the blindfolded Justitia is easily recognisable, and sculptures in the tympany. And at the rear of the building Atlas carries the world on his shoulders. No, it is not a very cheerful building!

The outside appearance of the town hall is glaringly different to the exuberant Baroque of the interior with its huge allegorical paintings and marble reliefs, derived from both the bible and from classical mythology. We must assume that the people of the time had no difficulty in understanding such picture stories, just as today we immediately grasp what a strip cartoonist means. For the Netherlands the high-ceilinged Burgerzaal is a rare example of a large non-religious architectonic space.

Power of Regents

Not everyone agreed with this plan. This town hall symbolised municipal politics. Power had fallen into the hands of a small number of families, closely related to each other, among them those of Pietersz. Cornelis Hooft, Reinier Pauw, Andries Bicker, Cornelis de Graeff and Coenraat van Beuningen. They formed a closed regents' clique, an oligarchy. Their town hall appeared to say: 'we're keeping the lid on the kettle, we're going our own way and we're keeping the people out.' The rulers of Amsterdam often carried out their own policy based on their business interests, a policy deviating from that of Holland. Holland, at it's turn, also often carried out its own policy within the Republic, without taking sufficient account of the other provinces. Justice was also administered in the town hall. Death sentences were carried out on the Dam. The people of the time were proud of the town hall. In a panegyric Vondel called it the 'eighth wonder of the world'. Henceforth the Nieuwe Kerk was also situated on the Plaetse. We must be thankful that the over-ambitious tower of Mayor Backer has not been built. The Nieuwe Kerk is prominent enough to maintain as a building next to the town hall.

Bartholomeus van der Helst's (1613–1670) Andries Bicker (1580–1652), merchant to Russia and Mayor of Amsterdam. (RMA)

Shipping-naval war

However, Amsterdam's prosperity was very vulnerable. The Republic and the upcoming trade nation England fought three naval wars against each other in the space of twenty years: 1652–1654, 1665–1667, 1672–1674. The Netherlands most famous admiral was Maarten Harpertszoon Tromp (born in 1598), a legendary fighter, whose seamen called him 'Bestevaer' (grandfather). He gathered fame against the pirates of Dunkirk. His biggest triumph was in 1639 when he beat the second Spanish Armada of the coast of the English harbour town Downs.

During the first naval war with the English Maarten Harpertszoon Tromp was killed near Ter Heide in 1653. When Michiel Adriaanszoon de Ruyter, who was second in command at the battle, climbed on board the flagship and saw the dead Bestevaer lying there, he said "Ah, If only I had died for him". The English now carried a broom at the masthead as a symbol that they had swept away the Dutch and now controlled the seas. It was some months before the fleet returning from the East Indies could put into port. In those days money was only in the form of coins and it was scarce. There was no reserve supply. Loans and mortgages had to be paid promptly. Rembrandt's lack of cash was typical. He had invested his money in his art business. Due to the crisis of 1653 art fell acutely in value and Rembrandt's financial difficulties increased. Bankruptcies, unemployment and a growing dissatisfaction of the people resulted. The Treaty of Westminster was concluded just in time. The fleet sailed into port and the city breathed again.

Free passage through the Oresund remained a priority for Amsterdam. Sweden could not be allowed to take over the Danish side of the Oresund. The Amsterdam envoy, Coenraat van Beuningen warned, the Swedish king with the words: "The keys to the Oresund – which are the warships – lie in the IJ". He gave the Danish king money from his own pocket to fit out a fleet. Amsterdam would thus help the weak Denmark against an attack from the Swedes. In the Northern War that followed, the Republic sent a fleet under De Ruyter in 1658 to support the Danes. De Ruyter was victorious and the Oresund remained open.

Michiel de Ruyter was born in Vlissingen in Zeeland in 1607 and after 1655 he lived on the Buitenkant in Amsterdam, at what today is the Prins Hendrikkade 131. He was the first to hold fleet manoeuvres in peacetime, so that he could command his ships in the same disciplined way that a land army could be commanded. Communication was by means of flag signals. How beautiful the three-masters were; how elegant the new, slimmer and faster type of ship, which put the Netherlands a step ahead of her competitors; how rich the colonial cargoes; more than enough for everyone, one might think. And how ridiculous the three naval wars with England now seem to us, the wars of 1652–1654, 1665–1667 and 1672–1674, which turned the North Sea into a mass grave for three-masters. National zeal? We should not let our imaginations run away with us. All too often the seamen were recruited in taverns because they had accepted a pint of beer from the recruiting officer, who then explained it was an acceptance of bounty money. The next morning the bailiff's rogues would haul the man from his lodgings. But his seamen loved Michiel de Ruyter. After Tromp he was given the honourable name of 'Bestevaer'. De Ruyter did not pocket the money intended for the crews' provisions. His wife personally ensured that proper provisions were purchased, which meant the crews suffered less from scurvy.

After the Four Day naval battle in 1666 the French envoy (who was allowed to be present as an observer) wrote to his king, Louis XIV, that he wanted to go and congratulate the admiral on his victory. He visited him in his cabin on board the flagship *De Zeven Provinciën*, but could not find him. He only came across a man with a broom in his hand, clearing up the debris. It was De Ruyter himself.

Jurrian Jacobson's Michiel Adriaensz. de Ruyter and his family (1662). (RMA)

So the 'terror of the great oceans' remained as simple as a legend of ancient Rome.

The greatest triumph of the fleet under the command of de Ruyter was the voyage to Chatham in June 1667 during the second English war. In the Medway, a branch of the Thames, the English fleet was destroyed. The English flagship the Royal Charles was captured (we must not forget, however, that at the time London was suffering from a plague epidemic). After this the peace treaty of Breda was signed.

The Flourishing of Zaanse Industry

Amsterdam had its industries, such as cartography and printing, and its sawmills constructed in 1658 on 26 bastions. However, the supply industries for shipbuilding and the finishing industries for imported goods flourished in the Zaanstreek, which was an offshoot of the Amsterdam harbour.

Here, in the second half of the seventeenth century, a region with the most versatile economic structure in the Netherlands was created. There were industries directly concerned with shipping, such as sawmills, shipbuilding, textile industries and rope-makers. Furthermore, there were other industries indirectly connected, such as biscuit bakeries, linen bleachers, the oil and paper industries, and salt extraction. For a few pounds per year the local inhabitants could acquire 'the legacy of the wind'. The first sawmill, *Het Juffertje* dated from 1596, the first paper mill, *De Kauwer*, was built in 1616. There were beam sawyers, oil mills, hulling mills, mills for stripping bark off trees, and snuff mills. For the paint industry there was white lead (also known as 'blauwsel') and paint mills. They had characteristic names such as *De Held Josua*, *De Grauwe Hengst*, *De Pronker*, *Het Gruyswijf*, *De Bijekorf*, and *De Eendracht*.

Amsterdam and Oranje

The Golden Age is permeated by the insoluble conflict between Oranje and the regents, particularly those of Amsterdam. A few years after the murder of Prince William the Grand Pensionary (secretary), the legal advisor of the States of Holland, Johan van Oldenbarnevelt, had pushed the young Prince Maurits forward as the new viceroy. In Oldenbarnevelt's opinion the viceroy should be the servant of the States, but the Prince was also Captain-General of the Union and that was a formidable power base. States and Prince both had power, but neither power was delineated. The legitimacy of the States was rooted in ancient city rights, and they recognised no sovereign power over them. Opposed to this was the legitimacy of the Oranje right of succession. In the eyes of the ordinary people Oranje was the selfless leader who epitomised the unity of the country, as opposed to the Holland and Amsterdam politics of self-interest. (In the meantime, Friesland had acquired its own vicere-

Windmills dominate the bulwark of the city. Drawing by Jan van der Heyden.

gal house, descended from William of Orange's brother, Jan van Nassau, nicknamed the Old). There was no mechanism in place to solve a conflict between these two principles of legitimacy. Two parties could exist side by side: those disposed towards the States and those disposed towards the Prince. If they were opposed to each other, only violence could solve such a conflict.

Religion and state

In 1610 a religious conflict broke out concerning Calvinistic doctrine. The theologian Arminius did not take Calvin's teaching literally, but explained it liberally or 'rekkelijk' (flexible). His adherents wrote a *remonstrance* concerning this insight, from which their name of Remonstrants is derived . Opposing him was Gomarus, who was 'precise' in doctrine and countered by writing the *Counter Remonstrance*. The regency was essentially flexible, the general masses remained adherents to 'precise' doctrine. Viceroy Maurits openly chose the side of the 'precise' party.

The theological dispute now intensified into the political question of who had the final say – the regents or the viceroy. On Oldenbarnevelt's initiative Holland took its own soldiers into service, a provocation that Prince Maurits, as military commander of the Union, could only regard as a coup d'état. He sacked the illegal soldiers and proceeded with his retinue to the council of Amsterdam where he sim-

Johan van Oldebarneveldt (1547–1619), government attorney of Holland. Etching by C.J. Visscher. (Atlas van Stolk)

ply removed the sitting magistrate. To the eighty-year-old burgomaster Cornelis Pieterzoon Hooft, Maurits spoke the words: "Farewell, for now it must be so. The need and service of the Land demand it." The confrontation had ended good-naturedly. In his long poem *Roskam* Vondel, a fervent Remonstrant praised the dismissed burgomaster, including the famous words:

> *'Hoe heeft hem Amsteldam ervaren wijs en simpel:*
> *Een hoofd vol kreuken, een geweten zonder rimpel"*

Matters went less well for Johan van Oldenbarnevelt, who was the optimisation of the party disposed towards the States. After a show trial he was condemned to death and beheaded at the Binnenhof. The Remonstrants had lost the battle, but in Amsterdam their worship was

tolerated in 'secret churches', such as De Rode Hoed (The Red Hat), a church secreted behind a milliner's premises. In 1980 De Rode Hoed found a fitting destiny as a cultural centre.

Because a number of Van Oldenbarnevelt's supporters were imprisoned in the castle of Loevestein, the party supporting the States was henceforth known as the 'Loevestein faction'.

William II, Civil War?

The Treaty of Munster clearly illuminated the impasse in the Dutch form of government. The treaty was a triumph for Amsterdam politics, but a curse for viceroy Willem II, because cutbacks in the army were now possible, which would undermine its function and its power. The Amsterdam business sense was opposed to excessive military expenditure. Once again it appeared that there was no mechanism in place to

Bartholomeus van der Helst (1638–1698), the rifleman's meal on the occasion of signing the Peace of Munster in 1648. (RMA)

Artus Quellinus de Oude, bust of Johan de Witt. (Dordrechts Museum)

solve such a political conflict. Therefore violence was used. In 1652 Willem II planned an attack on Amsterdam. His army was already stationed at the Gooi. Civil war! But Amsterdam made the best of a bad job, as befitted good businessmen. The literalist Andries Bicker resigned from the college of burgomasters. However self-confident the citizen-kings were, when it came down to it Orange had the charisma that gave it ascendancy.

Willem II died unexpectedly in 1652. His wife gave birth to her son, who would become Willem III, after his death. So began the first period without a viceroy, and it was dominated by the genius of Johan de Witt, progeny of a Dordrecht regent family, but married to Wendela Bicker, the daughter of the Amsterdam burgomaster. Under de Witt the Republic became a great power, which played a key role in the ever-changing European game of hegemony and equilibrium. Just as the Dutch of the Twentieth century owe their independence to a situation in which nobody begrudged us – England did not want Spain or France at the mouth of the Rhine, Maas and Schelde – so for twenty-two years de Witt maintained European equilibrium in a broader sense: in the Oresund, in the Channel, in the Mediterranean Sea, in the sea routes to the East and West Indies. This tiny country controlled European politics. That could not remain so for very long.

The Year of Disaster: 1672

In the disastrous year of 1672 the Republic was attacked by England and France and by both neighbouring German states, the bishoprics of Munster and Cologne. Due to the one-sided attention for the battle at sea with England, Johan de Witt had underestimated the French danger and neglected his army. Johan de Witt and his brother Cornelis now paid the price for the unsolved conflict between the competing principles of legitimacy. There was no mechanism to replace them legally. They were lynched by a mob in The Hague, while Willem III stood idly by.

Amsterdam was now in a difficult situation. The city had worked together with De Witt for twenty years, but Burgomaster Van Beuningen, as an envoy in France, had often enough warned of the French danger. De Ruyter had publicly defended Cornelis de Witt against the smear campaign directed at him. When he was told it was imprudent to do so De Ruyter answered: “If now in the fatherland men may not speak the truth things have reached a pretty pass, nevertheless I shall speak it, as long as my eyes are open.” De Ruyter might have served De Witt, but he was also indispensable to the house of Orange. He saved the country at the naval battles of Schooneveld and Kijkduin against the combined fleets of England and France. He became the symbol of the Fatherland. Amsterdam survived the crisis.

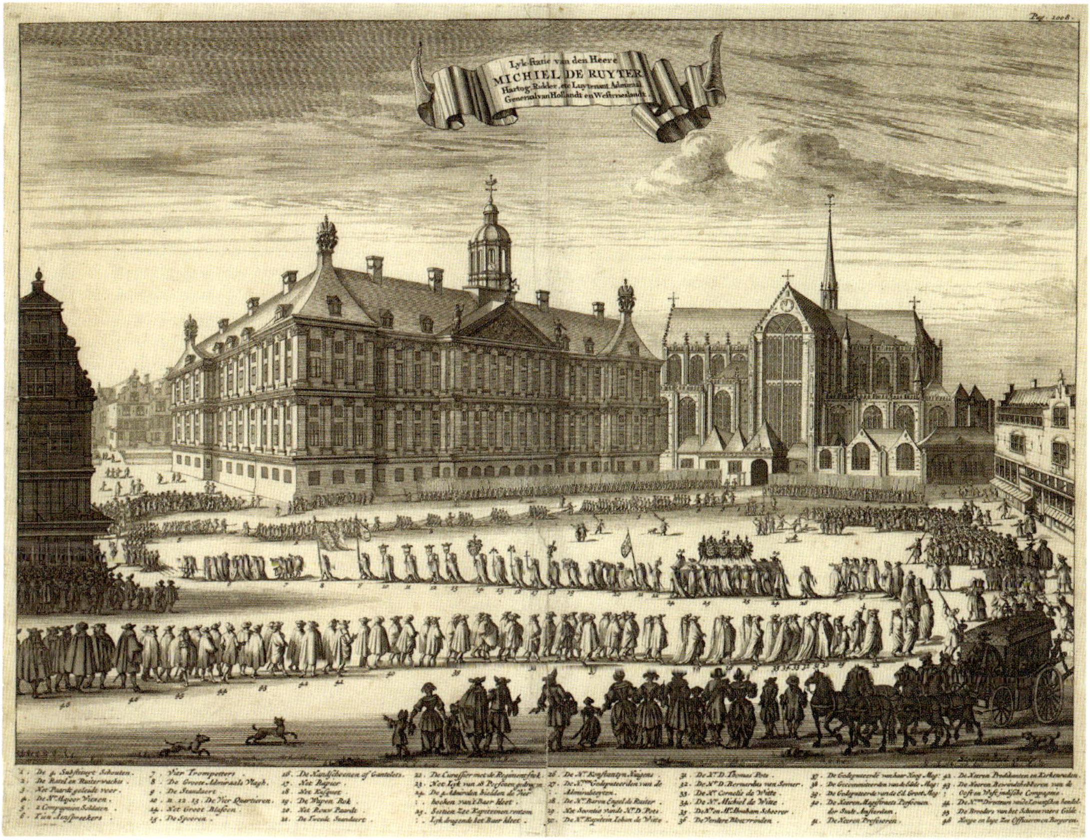

Michiel de Ruyter's funeral procession in 1677. This illustration informed all participants on the Dam. (GAA)

De Ruyter dies

When the immediate danger to the fatherland had abated, Willem III wished to extend the war to a greater European stage for his own dynastic interests. However, Amsterdam, true to tradition, opposed the costs of such a military adventure. The Prince himself spoke of 'ces coquins d'Amsterdam' (the wretches of Amsterdam). Van Beuningen fell into disfavour. In 1676 it was necessary to send a fleet to the Mediterranean to support Spain against France. De Ruyter knew that the old enemy Spain had a large fleet, but would certainly not come to his assistance; he also knew that the French ships were now bigger than in the year of disasters. He expressed his dissatisfaction about the poor condition of the Dutch fleet. But when those high in authority told him that "You begin to be afraid in your old age and are losing your courage", he gave his famous answer: "[...] it is my sorrow that the Lords have so corrupted and risked the flag of the State. But [...] where the Lord States trust their flag, I shall risk my life". Fate struck. Near Sicily a French sharpshooter wounded De Ruyter in the leg. He subsequently died of gangrene. De

Ruyter was buried with great honour in the Nieuwe Kerk. The sculptor Rombout Verhulst carved his mausoleum.

The half moon completed

In 1658 a start was made on the completion of the semi-circular ring of canals. Daniël Stalpaert drew the map on which a wall with 26 bastions after the French model encircled the city – in modern terms from the Haarlemmerplein to the Funenkade. The bastions were crowned with many windmills – it must have been a fantastic sight. Only the windmill on the Funenkade remains. The three main canals were extended across the Amstel to the IJ.

After the war of 1672 the elan, both economic and demographic, was broken. There were too few private buyers for the land and therefore

The 'Middelwegh', facing the old Muiderpoort, before 1769. (GAA)

large parcels were sold for a symbolic sum of money to charitable institutions, which can still be found to the east of the Amstel, such as the Amstelhof and the present-day Saphatihuis. In 1682 a rectangular area of more than 33 hectares between the Herengracht (now Nieuwe Herengracht) and the Muiderpoort – the Plantage – was set aside for allotments and a recreational area. On the other side of the city, to the west of Prinsengracht, the Jordaan was created, the streets of which followed the existing ditches and paths. It was not a consciously designed district, and did not link up organically to the canal plan. As the Lastage had formerly grown, the Jordaan grew steadily through the influx of newcomers and adventurers, who over the course of time were attracted by interests within the city.

H. G. ten Cate, the tower lock with the Jan Rodepoortstoren. (RMA)

Coenraat van Beuningen, mysticism and power united in one person. (GAA)

Coenraat van Beuningen

Beneath the fast-growing external magnificence of the Republic, a world of struggle and unassimilated ideas lay hidden, a leftover from the fermenting years of the Reformation. This opposition was epitomised by the Amsterdam burgomaster's son, burgomaster and versatile envoy, Coenraat van Beuningen (1622–1693). For a number of years as a young man he was under the influence of the Rijnsburg Collegiate, a sect that predicted world apostasy and poverty. He was a genius at languages and a great diplomat. Once at the court of Louis XIV he was announced as 'the Marquis of Buningen' (sic), because a guest was required to have a title. At this the proud Amsterdammer replied: "I am not a Marquis, Sire, I am the Burgomaster of Amsterdam." But for all his worldly skills he could not compete against the influence of mysticism and heresy, which predicted world apostasy and heralded the Thousand-year reign. *Esse, non videri*, was his motto: "Be, don't seem to be". His manic artistic spirit, however, was sober and opulent, mystic and rational, modest and powerful, dazzlingly successful and longing for meditation. How could he be *one* of these things without having the feeling that for each character trait he exposed, he was subverting another, truer self?

So the swift development of our Golden Age was compounded in him. In him it also fell apart. He fell into disfavour with the Oranges and in 1686 lost his post as burgomaster. He became insane and was shut up in his own large house at the Amstel 216. Nevertheless he continued to send a stream of improving pastoral letters into the outside world. At nights he escaped his guards, ran into the street in his nightgown, and warned his neighbours of a 'great fire above Frankfurt', announcing the end of time. In mental confusion he left his mark on the natural stone facade. In 1953 you could still clearly see in rust-coloured letters and lines the names Van Beuningen and Jacoba (his wife), various Hebrew letters and cabalistic signs such as octograms, formed by the diagonals of a regular octagon, and finally a number of three-masters, East Indies ships with flags.

Within the space of ten years several great figures of the Golden Age died: Rembrandt in 1669, Pieter Post in 1669, Johan de Witt in 1672, Vermeer in 1675, Michiel de Ruyter in 1676, Spinoza in 1667, Philip Vingboons in 1678, Vondel in 1679. Not long afterwards they were followed by Swammerdam in 1680, Constantijn Huygens in 1687, Coenraat Van Beuningen in 1693, Christiaan Huygens in 1695 and Justus Vingboons in 1698. Perhaps it was coincidence, but the Golden Age was over.

Rembrant's Elsje Christiaens, the eighteen year old Danish girl who killed her hostess with an axe after she couldn't pay the rent. On May the first 1664 she was sentenced to strangulation whilst tied to a pole on the Dam, after which they hung her body in the Volewijk in Amsterdam-Noord, the axe beside her. Rembrandt drew her on the day of her execution, for which he had to have gotten onto the IJ in a boat.
Dr. I. H. van Eeghen wrote: ´It's as if he was ahead of his time again: it is not horror but compassion that one can see in the depiction of the somewhat foolish sanguine eighteen year old Elsje.'
History does not answer the question how the girl, who had only been in Holland for two weeks, made herself clear. And, one is inclined to think with hindsight, did the fact that the two women could not understand each other not contribute to the irritation between them? Nobody bothered two ask Elsje. (GAA)

Rembrandt van Rijn 1606–1669, the Frans Banning Cocq corps, better known as the 'Night Watch' (1642). On the foreground we see the two leaders of the Amsterdam Riflemen: Frans Banning Cocq, lord of Purmerlandt, the man with the authoritative gesture and his lieutenant Frans van Ruytenburch, lord of Vlaerdingen in his golden suit. Interesting detail is the fact that the new Bourgeoisie (Ruytenburch's father had come to Amsterdam as a hawker from Bremen) had given themselves titles that belonged to medieval aristocracy. (RMA)

The Enlightenment Dawns 1700–1813

Chapter 4

Nicholaas Witsen and Tsar Peter the Great

(p. 76)
Cornelis Troost, Fun at the Amsterdam fair, disturbances at the 'beurstrommelen' (1746). (GAA)

At the end of the Seventeenth-century there was a certain repose in the Republic. Amsterdam no longer required its own deviant policy. Viceroy William III had a good relationship with the Amsterdam burgomaster and diplomat Nicolaas Witsen (1641–1717), only 19 years younger than Van Beuningen. When Willem III became King of England in 1688, Nicolaas Witsen was involved in the preparations. William III (1672–1702) was champion of the political balance in Europe. He feared the French' hunger for power which threatened the protestants in Europe. This eventually led to the war of Spanish Succession (1701–1713) in which William III led the anti-French coalition. This major European conflict was too much for the tiny country of the Netherlands. However, Willem III died unexpectedly in 1702 after falling from his horse. He had no children. The title Prince of Orange was now inherited by the Friesian side of the House of Nassau, descended from William of Orange's brother Jan de Oude. The States General, however, had had enough of the Oranges and their viceroys, having been at war under an Orange for thirty years. They named no successor, and so began the second period without a viceroy.

Nicolaas Witsen was a transitional figure, who once again epitomised the entrepreneurial passion and self-confidence of the Golden Age. Due to his experience with the Baltic trade he knew that the vast, unknown realm of Russia had great riches in timber, furs and grain and he travelled overland to Moscow in order to broaden commercial

Abraham Storck's drawing of the East-Indies ship *Peter en Paul*, on which Tsar Peter the Great had worked for four months. (GAA)

relations. He looked back on a century of amazing expansion and when he was thirty he wrote the first standard work on shipbuilding: *Old and modern-day Shipbuilding*. In 1697, through his friendship with Nicolaas Witsen, Peter the Great came to Amsterdam to study shipbuilding and cartography. At that time Amsterdam was still at the centre of the world. Witsen promoted the planting of Arabian coffee on Java and made great efforts to help the Huguenots, the French protestants driven out by Louis XIV. At the same time he lived through the almost silent decline of the Republic's role in European power play. To the Dutch he represents the rounding off of the Golden Age, the man who tried to gather together the assembled knowledge in books and collections.

The Treaty of Utrecht: 1713

In 1713, the Treaty of Utrecht brought to an end the enormously powerful role this small country, with Holland and Amsterdam as its pacesetters, had played in the previous century. Like the Treaty of Munster, this was the result of a great European conference, in which dynastic and territorial interests were weighed against each other, a political game from which the Republic was excluded. This was not unnatural. Although the Netherlands was one of the formal winners, the French negotiator made the following remark: "On traitera chez vous, sur vous et sans vous" – "We negotiate in your country, for your country and without your country." The small country had been shown it's place.

Dutch power had rested on the weakness resulting from internal conflicts in neighbouring countries and on our geographical position behind sandbars through which our small ships could find their way. Now, however, our neighbouring countries had put their houses in order and their ships had become larger. No ship of Holland could any longer oppose them. London and Hamburg assumed part of Amsterdam's role as a staples market, although the city still remained the world's financial centre. European rulers waged their costly wars with money which they borrowed in Amsterdam. The Deutz family controlled the German emperor's mercury mines and developed into one of the great banking houses. Bankers and people of independent means: this was the age of gentility. Since 1600 the classes had grown far apart. The regency families passed the profitable offices to each other. As a christening gift a new-born child might be offered a well-paid position. He then received the salary while a figurehead leased the position from him and did the work. There were heavy duties on the basic necessities of life. These duties were collected by tax lease-holders who, naturally, took the opportunity to enrich themselves. The decline of trade and industry meant that many people became unemployed. It was said that half the population lived on the charity of the other half.

On a number of occasions the Seventeenth century had witnessed the phenomenon of feverish speculation, in which tulip bulbs were sold and resold for high prices, a sort of 'pass the parcel' in which the last purchaser bore the loss. Since then speculation in worthless goods has figuratively been known as the 'tulip trade'. In 1720 in Amsterdam such speculation or 'soap bubble negotiation' was prevalent. On extremely loose grounds an enormous number of new enterprises were quoted on the stock market. The share prices rose to unprecedented heights. The East India Company share rose from 500 to 1200, that of the West India Company from 40 to 400. The exchange was to small to house all the speculators, so they moved to the Quincampoix coffee house in the Kalverstraat. Share prices rose so quickly that dealers could not spare themselves the time for other more personal 'business', but did this in a corner of the room. The virtuous, or at least god-fearing, common citizen was shocked by the huge amounts that were gambled. An angry mob plundered the coffee house.

A New Bourgeoisie

A new class, the middle class, was created between the rich and poor. In 1742 a list of 12,655 inhabitants of Amsterdam with an annual income of more than 600 guilders was drawn up for a tax assessment. A small group had an income of more than 16,000, but between that top amount and the lower limit of 600, was a large middle bracket of

Speculation in stocks in the coffee-house Quincampoix. (GAA)

bookkeepers, surgeons, merchants, shopkeepers, innkeepers and carpenters.

Here the new middle class announced itself. These were people who earned enough money to be able to buy a book with ideas of English or French origin, and who had learned enough to be able to read such a book and to empathise with the rise of eighteenth-century philosophy and natural sciences, the standard bearers of the Enlightenment. New ideas were stirring throughout the entire European continent. If there were natural laws for the planets following their elliptical courses round the sun, for an apple falling from a tree, or for the boiling of water, then it followed that God cannot change anything. God may have created the world, but after the deed of creation he was no longer almighty. In other words: God cannot stop the sun if Joshua wishes to enter the city of Jericho. That story is a legend. People must dare to use their own intelligence.

The Doelists

Like God, the king must also submit to the introduction of a constitution, which he would also be subject to. This new bourgeoisie wished to exert influence and have an element of power. Fumblingly, they sought forms of participation and democracy. The new citizens were oppressed by the regents and therefore in the Oranges they saw their natural ally. In 1747 they pressed for Willem IV, offspring of the Frisian branch of Nassau, to be given hereditary power. The Oranges, therefore, acquired royal dignity for the first time since Willem of Oranje had just missed out on the royal title. In Amsterdam they organised themselves into the Doelist movement under the leadership of porcelain merchant Daniël Raap. This movement derived its name from their meeting place Kloveniersdoelen, a shooting club. The demanded that the abuses the corrupt regents' clique were guilty of were to be stamped out, as well as far-reaching democratisation. During a visit to Amsterdam the Doelists managed to charge into the bedroom of the viceroy in order to make him sign a democratically favoured statement, but William IV refused. But William IV failed to seize the opportunity to modernise the constitution and so make the new bourgeoisie his ally.

The tax leaseholders revolt of 1748

The Doelists, however, were surpassed on the left by a radical popular movement, which resounded throughout the whole region of the Seven Provinces, the revolt of 1748 against the tax leaseholders. We have an eyewitness account of these events in Amsterdam in Chaim Braatbard's Yiddish chronicle, a modern translation of which has been published by L. Fuks. The plunderers had their own strict morality. The houses of the hated tax leaseholders were systematically plundered. Everything had to be destroyed. Those who were caught were consid-

In the night of the ninth of September 1748 the 'Doelists' visit Prince William IV, demanding a free and fair trial. Etches by Reinier Vinkeles. (Atlas van Stolk)

ered to be attempting to enrich themselves, and were thrown into the canal, spoils and all, and where left to drown. Immediately after the revolt three of its leaders in Amsterdam, including a woman, were sentenced to death. Braatbard relates: As soon as the three prisoners came out of the town hall, the drummers began their drum rolls [...] in order to prevent the people hearing the woman's screaming. But she screamed most pitifully: "Vengeance, vengeance, my dear citizens, stand by me. For now you allow me to die so shamefully, while I did not fight for myself. I fought for the whole country, against the tyranny of the tax leaseholders, who so tormented us citizens and who violently seized our money and possessions..." But, nevertheless, she had to hang. Suddenly people saw the pulley moving [...]. When she was hoisted out of the window of the Waag people heard her scream: "Vengeance, vengeance!" And so she hung out of the window and thrashed about until she was dead." What is remarkable is that the simple Jew Braatbard did not find this unusual. That's just how it was in those days.

The movement of reform was eliminated for years.

Patriots and supporters of the Prince

The troubles of 1748 were just the opening skirmishes. The ideas of the bourgeoisie still had to ripen. A generation later we find them back among the Patriots. Under this party name the citizens turned against the entire form of government of the Netherlands, against the regents as well as the house of Orange; and, moreover, against the dominant position of Holland and Amsterdam. All regions and cities were to

The tax leaseholders revolt of 1748, everything is thrown into the canals. (Atlas van Stolk)

Patriots plant the Freedom-tree on the Dam, the ideals of the French Revolution seemed within reach (1795). (GAA)

have equal rights. The leaders came from the country provinces for so long neglected. Daendels came from the Gelderland town of Hattem, Joan Derk came from der Kapellen and den Poll from Overijssel. After a number of incidents in 1787 many Patriots fled to France, which stood at the threshold of its great revolution. But they returned. In January 1795 a bitter frost had frozen the great rivers. The French armies under Pichegru occupied the Republic and brought the Patriots with them with their ideas of freedom, equality and fraternity. In Amsterdam the sitting city government was gently removed and replaced by 21 temporary representatives of the people. A Tree of Freedom was planted on the Dam. The people danced and could begin to experiment with democracy. Amsterdam had hardly grown since 1672, the population figure in 1795 was 217 000, the same as in 1672.

The Batavian Republic and the French Period

In the seventeenth century the Republic had missed out in the process of forming a state and in 1800 it was a completely obsolete house of cards. The democratic experiment could not immediately succeed in these circumstances. Therefore, in 1805 Napoleon appointed Rutger Jan Schimmelpenninck as monocratic ruler of the country. In 1806, however, Napoleon replaced him with his own brother, Louis, who was given the title King of Holland. In 1808, Amsterdam was the royal residence, the seat of government and the capital city of the country. The new king demanded the town hall for his residential palace; the city government moved to the Prinsenhof on the Oudezijds

Voorburgwal, where it remained until 1987. Louis Napoleon had the town hall rather barbarically rebuilt into habitable accommodation. And he had the small balcony – which is still there today – built on the first floor of his palace. He also wished to have the Waag demolished because it interfered with his view. His kingship, however, only lasted four years. In 1810 Emperor Napoleon dismissed his brother and incorporated the Netherlands into his Empire. Amsterdam was given the honorary title of third city of the Empire, after Paris and Rome.

In the collective memory the French period lives on in a different way than the German occupation. The period brought many improve-

Jacob Cats' drawing of the entry of the French in 1795. (GAA)

(p. 86-87)
Mattheus Ignatius van Bree, the entry of Napoleon In Amsterdam (1810). (AHM)

ments. The Netherlands began to catch up with the rest of the Empire, we learned to regard our country as a unity. In place of the many different regional measures and weights we adopted the metric system and we incorporated a land register and a uniform taxation system. The road to modern citizenship lay open, although Amsterdam played no special role in this great leap forwards.

The fact that the French exploited the country to the limit and that Napoleon forced our able-bodied men to take part in his fatal march to Russia, is less prominent in the national memory.

The Capital of a Kingdom, 1815 and onwards

Chapter 5

J. Paelinck's portrait of King William I. (Kon. Huisarchief Den Haag)

(p. 88)
Detail from Jacob Olie's Paleis van Volksvlijt at the Fredericksplein, 1892. (GAA)

The French left in 1813 and were replaced by a new king of Orange. The new constitution stated that the inauguration of a monarch must take place in Amsterdam. This recognition by the Oranges of Amsterdam as the capital city symbolised the reconciliation of the centuries-old dissent between them. The city allowed the monarch to use the old town hall as a palace. The Hague, however, remained the royal seat and centre of government. When Belgium became part of Dutch territory in 1815 the monarch of Oranje was given the title King William I. The government shuttled between The Hague and Brussels, and Amsterdam remained on the sidelines of power. However, in 1814 the Nederlandse Bank, successor to the Amsterdam Wisselbank of 1609, was established in the city and in 1831 the Nederlandse Handel Maatschappij (Netherlands Trading Company), which the energetic Willem I had founded in 1824, moved to Amsterdam.

After 1815 democracy grew steadily, although not without its ups and downs. Torbecke's constitution of 1848 enabled democracy and the hereditary monarchy to amalgamate into a manageable system. The King's power to govern the country was taken away by Torbecke: 'The ministers carry responsibility, the king is granted immunity'. Since then only the ministers could be held accountable by parliament, for their own policy but also for the sayings and doings of the King. The King, in his role as constitutional sovereign, was the symbol of the unity of the nation. Apart from a few conflicts in the first twenty years of the new constitution, there has been no question of conflicting principles of legitimacy. With a separate law Torbecke organised the administration of local government. They got a clearly defined autonomy. At the head of the local government stood the council. The daily administration of Aldermen was chosen by and

W. Hekking, the Goudsbloemgracht as seen from the Brouwersgracht to the Lijnbaansgracht. (GAA)

from the council. The mayor was chairman of the Aldermen and the council, but was appointed by the government. This was a prime example of Torbecke's art of administrative balance. Whilst the vote duly expanded from 1848 onwards, until in 1919 both men and women could vote, Torbecke's council-law help place without any considerable changes until 2002.

Slums

The French period had mangled Amsterdam into poverty and disrepair. Before the French occupation Amsterdam, with its 221000 inhabitants had been five times the size of Rotterdam and four times the size of The Hague. It was because of this that Amsterdam, after 1813, was in urgent need of repairs: houses, bridges and quaywalls were collapsing and suffering form decay, and the population was diminishing. The entrance to the IJ was silted up, ships could no longer be raised over Pampus by a ship's camel. In order to maintain a link with the sea William I had the North Holland Canal dug. But the new age of iron and steam did not yet take a grip on the city, the new prosperity had still to come.

The living conditions in the poor areas were atrocious. The owners of the old houses, often the lower middle classes, who had invested their savings, divided existing houses into one room apartments. They also built new houses on open courts which were then connected to the street by a 'hallway'. The slums did not have access to sunlight and fresh air. The council did not supply the streets with lighting, nor did they pave them, and the councils sewage carts did not come to collect buckets here. These buckets were thus emptied into the canals. There is and authentic account on the stench in the slums by J. G. van Niftrik B. Sc., who, from 1864 to 1901, had the leading position with the public sector. On the outset of his diaries in 1907 he wrote: 'You will not be able to make a clear enough picture of the uninviting and backward circumstances Amsterdam was in, as far as cleanliness and comfort was concerned'. On the occasion of his first guided tour of the Amsterdam slums, so he tells us, he fainted due to the overwhelming impenetrable stench. Worse than a fainting civil servant, however, were the epidemics like cholera that blighted the city form time to time. There was no sewer system until after 1900, and even then it only reached the newly built areas. Although many houses in the Seventeenth century had their own cesspit, nowadays a goldmine for archaeologists, the toilet was often situated above the canal. The canals were, in fact, the open sewers of the town. In the slums the so-called 'barrel system' was implemented: the barrel stood, ready for communal use, in the hallway or under the kitchen sink. Water was, in the first place, rainwater, and canal-side houses usually had a well. Next to this, since the

Eighteenth century, the 'Verschwater Societeit' (Freshwater Society) won water from the river 'Vecht' in barges. One barge contained 80000 litres of water, and one liter cost one cent. In 1846 the first cemented water-pipe that ran from the dunes to Amsterdam was taken into use. Amsterdam had a system of two waterworks: dune-water for consumption and Vecht-water for chores around the house, like cleaning windows. The first Rhine-water supply was taken into use in 1957. The water was first led to the dunes to be purified by the sand after which it came to Amsterdam.

Artis, Sarphati

In times of stagnating economy the impulse to modernisation could not come from the government. The first sign of recovery inspired by private initiative was the foundation of Artis in the Plantage by G. F. Westerman in 1838. Existing collection of animals were brought here. Artis was a private fellowship after Eighteenth century stan-

Jacob Olie, the Paleis voor Volksvlijt at the Frederiksplein, 1892. (GAA)

dards with an educational aim. It became a world famous centre for the study of nature. In 1939 it came into possession of the city. Improvement of the unhealthy living conditions came from the doctors. Nobody understood the necessity of hygiene. Semmelweis had yet to start his desperate battle in Vienna, against the unwashed hands of doctors and nurses. Robert Koch had yet to discover anthrax, and yet the doctors had a good hunch as to what was needed. Doctor Samuel Sarphati took initiative and founded a bread factory and started to implement regular garbage collection. Next to this he initiated the build of the 'Paleis voor Volksvlijt' (from 1864 to 1866) and the Amstel Hotel, the first major development outside the Singelgracht. Amsterdam's size was still dictated by Daniel Stalpaert's vision of 1658. The space within the ramparts with it's 26 bastions was full. Carefully the expansion began. First the bastions were taken apart, after which the long narrow belt was built, what is now the Marnixstraat, Weteringschans and Sarphatistraat. In 1866 van Niftrik designed a great plan for development outside the Buitensingelgracht, but this was turned down on the grounds that it was too luxurious. It would be a while before they had the courage to build outside the Buitensingelgracht.

Plantage and Vondelpark

At the start of the Eighteen-sixties Christiaan P. van Eeghen, another enlightened citizen. Took the initiative to establish the Vondelpark, for, in the east, the green area Plantage had been lost. When, in 1682, the Plantage was founded, the allotments were rented out. In these lots it was illegal to build either buildings for permanent use or a business or home. This rule, however, was broken frequently. Numerous permanent buildings had been built, with or without a licence. Around 1858 there were tea-gardens, inns pubs and a bathhouse, all of which could still be termed under recreational facilities. However, there was also a rice-husking mill, a mason's yard, a stained-glass factory, two shipyards, a florist, numerous shops and a livery stable, all of which were in clear breach with the 1682 zoning plan. Moreover, at the address which is now Plantage Middenlaan 27, there was a nursery. Since then other educational institutes have resided at this address, amongst which the Hervormde Pedagogische Academie and the IVKO-school. The existence of a nursery makes one wonder, in an area where officially nobody was allowed to live. In 1858 the council decided to make an end to this classic example of the policy of tolerance. They simply terminated the leases, which led to a tumultuous protest movement, for the illegal but tolerated investments would be lost. Eventually the tenants got the chance to buy their lots for a reasonable price. The canals which served as an open sewer were cleared and the council promised to

Vondelpark, design by J. D. and L. P. Zocher. (GAA)

Horse-drawn omnibus. The line Dam-Plantage existed between 1872–1883. (GAA)

provide the Plantage with modern cemented sewers. This time there was to be no working-class area, like the council had envisaged, but expensive private housing. This is how the area we know now came into being, with its fine late-Nineteenth century buildings. Only Artis, which took up 10 acres of the Plantage, stayed where it was.

The park which was built as compensation on the west side of the city, was designed in the English landscape-style by father and daughter Zocher. It was first used in 1864. The park got its peculiarly elongated form due to the subsequent expansions. This contributed hugely to the park's accessibility, and it joined areas, which were very different in character. Louis Roger unveiled the statue of Vondel in 1867, and this is were the park got it's name from. The Vondelpark was a popular succes. The Ronde Blauwe Theehuis, designed by H.A.J. Baanders in the 'Nieuwe Zakelijkheid' style, dates from 1937.

Housing Improvement

The population of Amsterdam grew from nearly 250000 in 1859 to 520000 in 1900; it was more than doubled in forty years. The first rapport that dealt with the bad public housing dates from 1853, but at

Artis'great aviary. (GAA)

the time the government was still too wrapped up in rigid liberalism which didn't allow any government intervention. Private charities had to take initiative. Before the Housing Act made public housing the government's responsibility there were seventeen private initiatives to improve public housing in Amsterdam. This wave of initiative was led by some inspired ladies from wealthy families; Helene Mercier (1839–1910), Johanna ter Meulen (1867–1937) and Louise Went (1865–1951). They had had training in England, and through this they learned that the poor could not be put into 'neat' housing just like that, it involved a whole learning process. This is why they implemented housing supervisors, who checked regularly to see if the house was kept tidy.

The canals in the Jordaan, which had turned into channels of waste, were seen as health hazards. Sanitation meant filling in the canals. The filling in of the Warmoesgracht-Rozengracht in 1895, which created the Raadhuisstraat, did not only serve public health, it also benefited the increasing traffic. However, people where to regret filling up the canals when health improvement had lost its urgency.

Many specific crafts which were typical for the lower-middle classes were lost to industrialisation. In an 1855 study of the Palmstraat, a small street in the Jordaan, Ruud Siekerman listed all of the following occupation in this one street: construction worker (in many variations), box-maker, corn-carrier and corn-counter, miller, miller's-help, mill-maker, nightwatch, pawnbroker, police officer, shoemaker, cigar-maker, porter, chair-caner, confectioner, rope-maker, workman, sawdust merchant, and sailor. The women had the following occupations: corn-measuring help, starcher, servant, wringer, milkmaid, seamstress, cleaner, barkeeper, peat-carrier, feather-searcher, fisherwoman, washerwoman, shopkeeper and charwoman. In 1890 the corn measuring was replaced by weighing the corn, the corn and saw-mills had been replaced by housing. The rope-maker had been mechanised and the nightwatch' duty had been taken over by the police. New occupations had arisen, like a clerk, and in the street there lived a supervisor of the Amsterdamsche Omnibus Maatschappij, founded in 1872. The first omnibus, which rode the Dam-Plantage route, was a smart diligence, pulled by two horses. The diligence was replaced by the horse-tram in 1883, and subsequently by the electric tram in 1902.

The Great Turnaround

The great turnaround in Amsterdam came in 1870. Trade was given an enormous impulse due to the opening of the Suez Canal in 1869, the establishment of German unity in 1870, and the liberalisation of trade with the Dutch East Indies. In 1870, the first cargo of raw dia-

L'ILLUSTRATION

JOURNAL UNIVERSEL

PRIX DU NUMÉRO : 75 CENTIMES
Collection mensuelle : **3** fr. — Volume semestriel : **18** fr.
Les demandes d'abonnement doivent être affranchies et accompagnées d'un mandat-poste ou d'une valeur à vue sur Paris au nom du Directeur-Gérant.

44e ANNÉE. — VOL. LXXXVIII. — N° 2267.
SAMEDI 7 AOUT 1886
BUREAUX : 13, RUE ST-GEORGES, PARIS

PRIX D'ABONNEMENT
PARIS & DÉPARTEMENTS : 3 mois, **9** fr.; 6 mois, **18** fr.; un an, **36** fr.
ÉTRANGER : Pour tous les pays faisant partie de l'Union postale :
3 mois, **11** francs ; 6 mois, **22** francs ; un an, **44** francs

LES TROUBLES D'AMSTERDAM

LE JEU DE L'ANGUILLE SUR LE LINDENGRACHT (CANAL DES TILLEULS) LE 25 JUILLET

Dessin fait sur place, par M. de Haenen, envoyé spécial de l'*Illustration*.

monds arrived in Amsterdam from South Africa, and the diamond industry began to flourish; people spoke of the 'Cape Age'. The North Sea Canal, which was opened in 1876, gave Amsterdam a direct link with the sea. The completion of the Central Station in 1889 made sure Amsterdam became part of a modern-day traffic network. The railway in the Nineteenth century was what the aeroplane would be in the Twentieth century.

At the end of the 19th century Amsterdam made great strides as far as big city allure was concerned. This occurred in the European style of that time, the so-called Neo-styles, in which elements of old European styles such as Gothic, Renaissance and Baroque could be seen. Since this time Central Station, the Victoria Hotel and the Sint Nicolaaskerk have marked the entrance (by rail) to the city. The Americain Hotel, the Hirsch building and the Stadsschouwburg characterise the Leidseplein. Besides the Stadschouwburg, cultural temples such as Carré, the Concertgebouw, the Stedelijk Museum and the Rijksmuseum were built. They wouldn't be expanded and renovated until a hundred years later.

A fierce debate, which hasn't abided in 2000, started on the build of the Central Station in the old harbour where the Amstel

(p. 98)
The 'Paling' revolt in the Jordaan, 1886. (GAA)

Gerrit Lambrechts, the Leidseplein and the Leidsepoort. To the right the theatre which burnt down in 1890. (GAA)

The Rijksmuseum by P.J.H. Cuypers (1885).

meets the IJ. Indeed, the station did cut off Amsterdam from the IJ. However, the invaluable advantage was that the old centre was spared mess of storage and pollution that often accompanied a modern harbour in the age of steam. Moreover, the old centre kept her vital function as *centre*. New harbours developed on the artificial islands that made up the Oostelijk Havengebied, which, after 1980, would become a residential area.

In the Nineteenth century Amsterdam had a tradition of performing music in the Felix Meritus and Parkzaal, situated in the Plantage opposite the Hortus. Brahms, on visiting Amsterdam in 1879, is known to have said: 'Ihr sied liebe Leute, aber schlechte Musikanten' (you are friendly people, but bad musicians). The Parkzaal, led by Willem Stumpff, was arranged with bar-tables, around which people drank and talked during the concert. The buffet in the concert-hall was a plague to people who wanted to quietly enjoy the music. The Parkzaal was broken down in 1882. A few city-loving patricians took the initiative for the foundation of the Concertgebouw on the west side of town, which was taken into use in 1888. Discipline reigned from the outset, the visitors weren't allowed to talk or drink during concerts and the musicians wanted to prove the spiteful words of Brahms wrong. The first conductor was Willem Kes, followed by Willem Mengelberg, who made the Concertgebouworkest famous around the world.

Amsterdam also experienced a flourishing period in literature and in the other arts. The Tachtigers profited from the educational reforms that Torbecke had implemented. Modern languages now got a prominent role in education. They incorporated a stream of foreign influences in their work, from Shelley to Zola. Breitner was the painter of the townscape of Amsterdam, as Jacob Olie was its pho-

The Parkzaal, with its café tables around 1860. (GAA)

tographer. The oeuvre of Jan Sluyters gave Amsterdam a clear insight into the many kinds of French painting, from he always absorbed the best. With Hermann Heijermans Amsterdam had a playwright whose plays were performed throughout Europe. *Op hoop van zegen* ('Hoping for the Best') was premièred in the Hollandse Schouwburg on Christmas Eve 1900. Heijermans had a preference for premières on 23 December because opinions of his play had gone round the city by word of mouth before *De Telegraaf* (Dutch newspaper) could slate his work.In 1877 the Athenaeum Illustre became a true university. Amsterdam was proud to fund such a great institution itself, it was only in 1969 that it was taken over by the state. The physicist L.H. van 't Hoff; J.D. van der Waals and P. Zeeman of the University of Amsterdam all won Nobel prizes. Hugo de Vries was world famous for his mutation theory, a major contribution to the science of genetics.

Furthermore, after 1870 the over-populated city broke through the restraining bonds of the Buitensingelgracht. A ring of new residential areas – Dapperbuurt, Oosterparkbuurt, the Pijp, Kinkerbuurt and Staatsliedenbuurt – was created. The laying out of the long narrow streets and the design of the houses were left to private initiative, so that the general interest was not to the forefront. These areas had a bad reputation, as far as quality and urban development was concerned.

Berlage

Idealistic liberal and socialist movements came about as a reaction to unfettered capitalism. Henri Polak organised the diamond workers into the General Diamond Workers Union (ANDB) of 1894, which became the core of the modern trade union movement.

H.P. Berlage designed the head office of the ANDP (1900) in the Henri Polaklaan, a building built like an Italian Renaissance fortress. In it there are wall-panels designed by R. N. Roland Holst. In these paintings he portrayed the exultation of the working class through solidarity. The paintings are supplemented with texts of his wife Henriette Roland Holst. Berlage thus became the founder of the New Architecture.

His main work is the Koopmansbeurs (commodity exchange) at the Damrak, which was completed in 1903. A building like that manifests itself as it is, and doesn't pretend to be elegant or graceful. The rigid shapes aren't obscured by fanciful decorations. Front

(p. 102)
The Concertgebouw's podium during the interval of the opening concert on April 11 1888. Drawing by N. van der Waay. (Concertgebouw Amsterdam)

The Beurs van Berlage, groundbreaking architecture by H. P. Berlage (1903).

statues aren't treated as independent pieces of art but play a subsidiary part in relation to the main design. They are integrated in the front, placed in corners, so that they wouldn't stick out. The Beurs' idealism and moralism makes it a child of its time. This is underlined by the texts under the tower clock: *Bijd uw Tijd, Duur uw Uur* (Bide Your Time), written by the poet Albert Verwey, and the wall-paintings of R. N. Roland Holst, Jan Tooroop and others. In these paintings labour is honoured, which brings forth the goods that are traded with at the Beurs. Now that the Beurs is used for

Drawing from 1887 of the Concertgebouw, still situated in the middle of a field. (GAA)

expositions and concerts everyone can enjoy this art in which the traditional crafts of sowing, harvesting and coal mining are glorified. Berlage was given the assignment to draw up an extension plan for the southern part of Amsterdam, to the south of the Lairessestraat-Ceintuurbaan, between the Schinkel and the Amstel.

Map of Berlage's expansion plan, Plan Zuid 1917. (GAA)

The Twentieth century up to 1945

Chapter 6

F. M. Wibaut, the founder of social housing in Amsterdam. (GAA)

(p. 106)
The Palace on the Dam, the Burgerzaal.

If a balance were to be made up of Amsterdam around 1900, one could conclude it to be a flourishing city. It had waterworks, gas, electricity, telephone and had made a start on the sewer system. The centre had been recently opened up by a traffic improvement, the Raadhuisstraat. The city had culture, a university, hotels and night-life, but it still hadn't solved its slum problem. This was the task of the coming century. The 1901 Housing Act created this opportunity.

The Housing Act, that went together with the Health Act, was in concurrence with the developments in other European countries around 1900With a view to creating better housing, some houses could be termed unfit to live in. Public housing could be subsidised through housing associations. Furthermore, it prescribed the preparation of an expansion plan as a precaution against land speculation. Housing Associations were created according to the sectarian dividing lines that then existed, such as Rochdale, De Dageraad, Het Oosten and Patrimonium. The municipality also took over social housing such as in the Zaanhof of 1918. F.M. Wibaut, the first social-democrat alderman commented: "Well, that's a start, and there'll be no stopping it!" Wibaut was a pragmatic socialist. He translated the Fabian essays, written by the couple Sidney and Beatrice Webb who wanted to realise socialism step by step, into Dutch. He had no ambition for national politics, local politics was where he could and wanted to work. Wibaut's tombstone reads the following epitaph: '*There is but one country-the earth, there is but one people-humanity, there is but one faith-love.*' In 1903 Henri Polak got into the council as the first and only social democratic member, from 1919 onwards they constantly formed the largest faction, with fluctuations from 21 seats in 1982 to 12 seats in 1990.

After the First World War the great period of city expansion and

Housing in the architectural style of the Amsterdam School.

social housing dawned. In 1921 S. Rodrigues de Miranda took over the public housing department from Wibaut. Berlage had designed the beautiful Zuid between the Amstel – the Berlage Bridge is named after him – and the Schinkel, where the Olympic Stadium was built in 1928. With his system of broad avenues, which enclosed smaller districts, it is both orderly and recognisable, a rare successful municipal plan. West, too, from the Stadium up to and including the Hoofdweg, was built between the two World Wars.

The architecture of these districts was governed by the Amsterdam School. They first manifested themselves with the Scheepvaarthuis in 19016, built by their leading lights Michel de Klerk, J. M. van der Mey and Piet Kramer. The Scheepvaarthuis was seen as a monu-

Housing in the architectural style of the Amsterdam School.

ment of the spirit as oppose to the sober nature of the Beurs van Berlage. The brick was a decorative drape over the frame of the building The bricks were artistically mortared and lavished attention was paid to the outside of the houses with many decorative stone , wrought iron and stained-g lass windows. Thus the building became one big sculpture.

The new style was an immediate success and was emulated in house construction. In the areas that are marked as the Ring '20-'40, one can see the arched fronts, round or hollow, the scalloped ridgepieces, the vertical tiles. Not to mention the special treatment of the windows; the complicated showy brickwork and the daring corner solutions. The corner could not just be an interruption of two walls but had to be absolved into roundings and serrations, by a towering bay or a real tower. Finally there were the wild porches, its doors adorned with wooden blocks and fanciful railings plus the almost illegible decorative house-numbers. Everywhere in the city one can see the ornaments of stone and wrought iron, on the bridges of Piet Kramer; complicated railings, grinning sea monsters or honest labourers. These architects weren't any less idealistic than Berlage. They, like Berlage, were inspired with the thought of exulting the people, by providing them with beautiful houses and a beautiful area to live in. the climax of the public housing of Michiel de Klerk is the triangular block Het Schip between the Zaanstraat and the Oostzaanstraat, dating from 1920. In the corner of Het Schip, near the Spaarndammerplantsoen, there used to be a small post-office, which, in 1999, became a museum for the Amsterdamse School under the name of Het Schip.

Another characteristic design by Michiel de Klerk is the Vrijheidslaan, between the Wolkenkrabber and the Berlagebrug. The façade's of the Vrijheidslaan are treated as one whole, reminiscent of the goal of the Amsterdamse School. After de Klerk's early death in 1923 – he was only 39 – the second faze of the Amsterdamse School developed, which kept all the general features but became more quite, like for instance the Minervalaan.

The managing director of public housing, Arie Keppler, created the famous 'garden villages' Betondorp, Nieuwendam and Oostzaan, in which, because of the socialist ideal, pubs weren't allowed and churches were sparse as well. The style is again a variant of the Amsterdamse School. Noord, which traditionally felt itself left out, not only got the garden village Vliegendorp but also the Vliegenbos, which was predestined to become a 'wild forest'.

In the twenties the slums in Uilenbrug and Valkenburg in the old Jewish quarter were renovated. The Jordaan was also on the list for an

Housewives with buckets of faeces at the 'Boldootwagen'. (GAA)

extensive renovation. Many houses were small, low and dark, couldn't be ventilated and did not have a tap or a toilet. The inhabitants had to make use of a bucket. These were collected by a 'bucket-cart', which was sneeringly referred to as the 'Boldootwagen', after a well known perfume factory of the time. If these carts couldn't get to the houses, the bucket was simply emptied into the canal. The bucket-cart was laid out with a charcoal-fire to neutralise the stench, In the Jordaan one could always buy a little fire in the shape of burning charcoal, in the many water and fire shops. However, the world-wide crisis of 1929 put an end to the ambitious renovation. In 1934 they demolished 107 houses without a toilet and 68 walled-in houses, adjacent to a sunless court. Gradually the sewer system spread through the city. On 31 December the Boldootwagen rode its last round through the city.

The Stadsschouwburg was the most important theatre in the country. An international repertoire was performed here, such as Wedekind, Tsjechov, Ibsen, Maeterlinck, and this attracted audiences from all over the world. Whilst the socialist Herman Heyermans was struggling with his talent and his lack of funds, the Stadsschouwburg was not granted him but two artists with which he had nothing in common, his adversaries Edward Verkade and Willem Royaards. They both adhered to the idealist art of the Nineteen hundreds, both convinced that theatre should not be realistic, but stylised, and the director had a determining role. Verkade was strict and sober, searching for mystique in the tradition of William Morris and Gordon Craig. Royaards, who likened to the mass-theatre of Max Reinhardt, was the artist of the grand gesture and beautiful words. After them Albert Defresne and Albert van Dalsum tried to bring engaged theatre in the thirties, choosing to reflect the problems of the time. Next to the Stadsschouwburg the Paleis voor Volksvlijt was a theatre in which Heijermans performed his drama. This building of steel and glass burnt down in 1929.

The idea that art was a common good which couldn't financially exist on its own had led to subsidy, but wasn't yet structurally acknowledged. The alderman Emanuel Boekman of Amsterdam saw the necessity of researching and setting down the government's responsibility for art as a general rule. He obtained his doctorate in 1939 on the dissertation 'government and art', which, after 1945, would as a blueprint for the art politics of Amsterdam.

The General Expansion-plan

In 1921 the area of Amsterdam was almost quadrupled by the annexation of neighbouring agricultural municipalities. To fill these newly-annexed areas the city government wanted to have an expansion plan

ALGEMEEN UITBREIDINGSPLAN VAN AMSTERDAM.

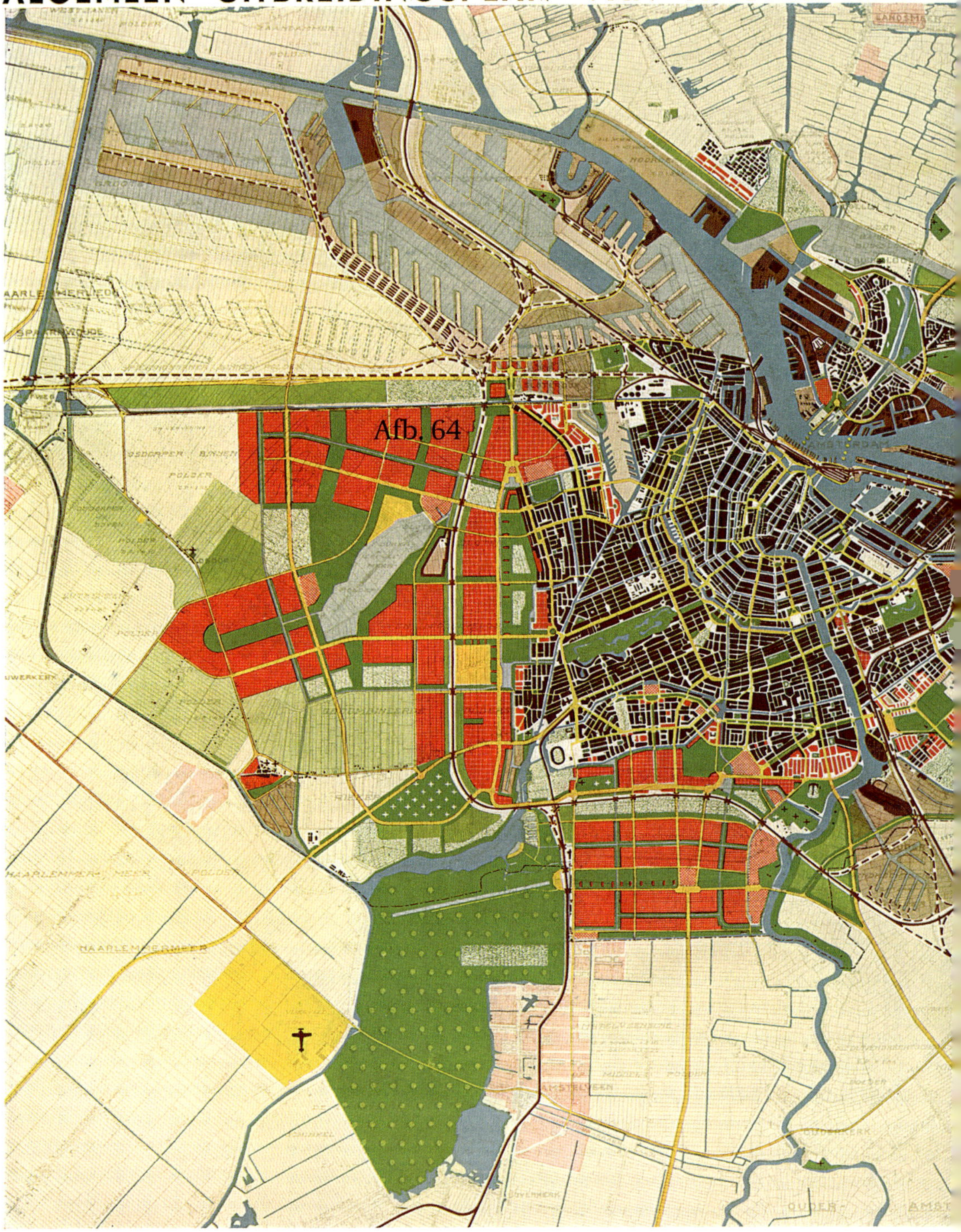

BIJLAGE VAN HET BOUWKUNDIG WEEKBLAD ARCHITECTURA VAN 23 MAART 1935, No. 12.

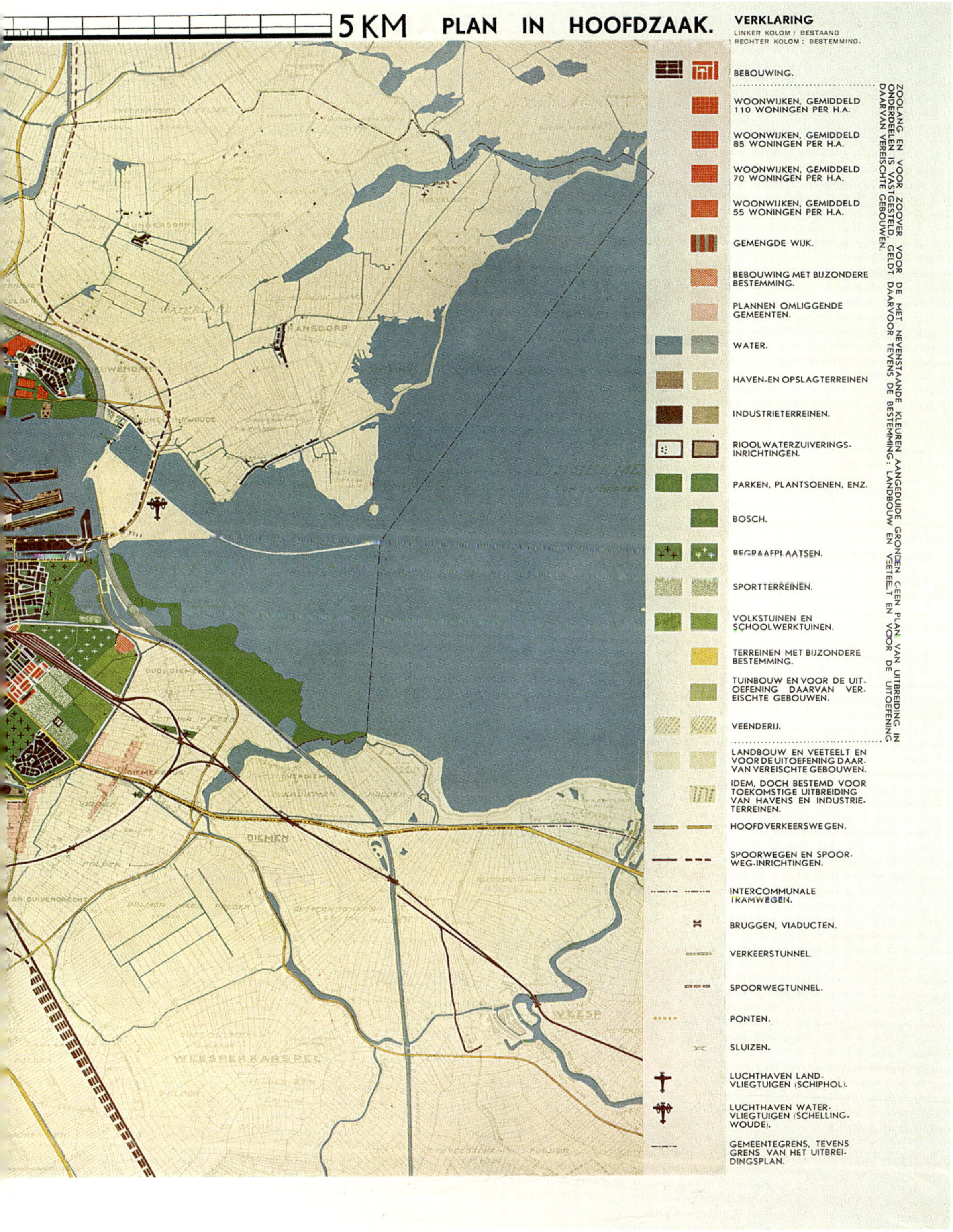

Map of the General Expansion Plan of Amsterdam in the thirties (AUP) by Cornelis van Eesteren. (GAA)

drawn up, a plan that would not be a partial plan, but one that would take the city as a whole as its point of departure. A City Development department was added to the Public Works Service and in 1928 C. van Eesteren became its head. His appointment resulted in the international ideas of De Stijl, Bauhaus and the New Objectivity, which differed radically from the romantic Amsterdam School, making their appearance in the city. The General Expansion Plan (AUP) appeared in 1935. It looked forward to what was then still far in the future – the year 2000. This plan took the principles of the Public Health Act very seriously. Too often during the previous hundred years cheap public housing had been built in places, literally, beneath the smoke of unhealthy industries. The AUP distinguished between the functions living, working, traffic and recreation and ensured light, fresh air and space. In place of the traditional blocks, in which the flats had unequal sunlight, the open method of strip building was introduced. To the west side of the garden villages the Sloterplas was drawn, which would be created by digging up the Slotermeerpolder. Space and nature were the themes, Traffic was not to hinder the area. This is why they did not consider traditional streets, but strips of housing on both sides of the main traffic arteries.

The execution of this plan could only be taken in hand after the Second World War, but the fact that the plan existed had an immediate favourable effect. Land speculation was avoided and Amsterdam was spared the creation of messy suburbs and slum areas or 'bidonvilles' (shantytowns) which mar the immediate surroundings of so many of the world's great cities.

In 1926 the small airfield of Schiphol, far away in the Haarlemmermeer polder, became the Municipal Airport. In 1928 the council decided to follow up a plan, which had already been proposed years before by Jac. P. Thijsse, namely, the creation of the Amsterdamse Bos (Forest of Amsterdam), 900 hectares in area, which was to be constructed on the south-west side of the city.

World crisis

The élan of the twenties was destroyed by the crisis of 1929. Prices collapsed, wages and social benefits fell, unemployment increased alarmingly, even though there was still necessary work to be done. Remarkable features were the incomplete building sites in the new residential areas and the numerous To Let signs outside empty houses. Because of the poverty young people lived with parents for a longer period of time and marriage plans were postponed. In July 1934 a reduction in unemployment benefit led to serious public order disturbances in the Indische neighbourhood, the Jordaan and Kattenburg, among other places. In 1917, Jac. P. Thijsse had argued for the planting of a wood to the south west of Amsterdam. The council agreed to this in 1928, and, because of the crisis, this relief work had to combat unemployment The polder land had to be prepared by raising it and by laying a drainage system. Consider the teacher, sacked for reasons of economy, who was suddenly forced to carry out excavation work – and don't even ask about wages which consisted merely of support. Future generations looked back on this with astonishment.

HET LEVEN
GEILLUSTREERD
BUREAUX VAN REDACTIE EN ADMINISTRATIE
KEIZERSGRACHT 268 AMSTERDAM

HET OPROER TE AMSTERDAM.

Revolt in the Jordaan, 1934. (GAA)

War

In the early morning of 10 May 1940 Adolf Hitler's Germany attacked the Netherlands. Queen Wilhelmina and her ministers went to London to continue the struggle from there. They still bore responsibility for the colonies in the East and West Indies and for the merchant fleet insofar as it was at sea. Rotterdam was bombed on 14 May, and the next day the Dutch army decided to surrender.

In 1940 Amsterdam had 800,000 inhabitants. The city had suffered little immediate damage during the five-day battle. In the five years of occupation, however, the city suffered in a number of allied air raids, particularly north Amsterdam where the Fokker factories (Dutch Aircraft manufacturers) were situated. As a result of inaccurate bombing 267 people were killed in this district.

The city council did not know what attitude to adopt to the occu-

A view of Amsterdam during the occupation, nazi's marching passed the Herengracht.

pying forces. It had happened so quickly and people were not mentally prepared for it. There was no protest when communist and Jewish members of the council were removed from office. This was not in accordance with the constitution but there was no one who stepped out of line and said: 'I resign as well, for what is such a city council worth?' Jewish civil servants were dismissed and only a few schools protested about the sacking of their Jewish teachers. Jewish teachers and students were also excluded from the university. When the Germans called up the Jews to be registered, most of them did so. The civil service showed itself unbelievably obedient and zealous, for instance in the preparation of a city map showing where Jews lived. Becoming aware of the necessity of resistance was a slow process.

Jewish Persecution

The first 'razzias' (round-ups) of Jews took place on 22 February 1941 in Waterlooplein, the heart of the old Jewish quarter. The assault vans drove up, the Germans jumped out, grabbed the men, beat them up; it was as if it were a hunt for vermin. Four hundred Jewish men were arrested and deported to Mauthausen where they were murdered. The answer of the people of Amsterdam to this razzia was the February strike of 25 and 26 February 1941. It was a unique occurrence that the non-Jewish population should stand up for its Jewish fellow-citizens. The Germans took ruthless measures. People were killed and death sentences pronounced. Amsterdam was forced to pay a heavy fine. The mayor and aldermen were dismissed, the city council abolished. The will of Amsterdam to resist was broken and remained broken for a long time.

The systematic deportations of the Jews began in July 1942. They were assembled in the Hollandse Schouwburg in the Plantage Middenlaan. From there they were taken to Westerbork from where trains left every week for the concentration camps in Germany and Poland.

Those who wished to avoid deportation had to cross over to England, as did the dismissed city council member Dr. Ben Sajet and his two sons; or try to reach Switzerland or Spain overland. You could also go into hiding, which for the majority of law-abiding Dutchmen, Jewish and non-Jewish, was not an easy decision to make. Punishment on discovery was severe. It was difficult to find suitable addresses. Groups of students in Amsterdam and Utrecht specialised in housing Jewish children – it was easier to find accommodation for children than it was for adults. Often parents would say 'we'll manage, as long as the child is safe'. Otto Frank went into hiding in a most unusual way. He had the back part of his house, behind his office at Prinsengracht 263, rebuilt into a hiding place for his family and a few friends. They moved in during the summer of 1942. Here Anne Frank

Jewish Neighbourhood: the entrance to the Nieuwe Kerkstraat, renamed Judenstrasse/ Joodschestraat (Jewish-street). Photo by J. Rotgans. (GAA)

The hunger winter of 1944–1945 caused many deaths.

The last great raid in Amsterdam Zuid and Oost, on June 20 1943. Photo take in the Uiterwaardenstraat on the corner of the Gaaspstraat. (GAA)

wrote her diary. Those hiding there, however, were betrayed and on 4 August 1944 they were arrested. Miep Gies saved Anne's diary. Otto Frank was the only one who returned. When reports of Anne's death reached Amsterdam, Miep gave him the diary. It was published in book form in 1947.

Resistance

In 1944 Amsterdam was the national centre of resistance. This resistance consisted of helping Jews, forging papers, removing personal

index cards from the municipal register, aiding English pilots and carrying out armed attacks on prisons and on Germans and their accomplices, and of preparing and distributing illegal newspapers and books. *Het Parool, Trouw, Vrij Nederland*, and De Bezige Bij (a publisher) all began life as illegal publications. The most famous resistance fighter was Gerrit van der Veen. He was arrested, sentenced to death and on 10 June 1944 he was executed by firing squad in the sand dunes near Overveen. Fritz Kahlenberg organised notable photographs in 'De Ondergedoken Camera' (The Hidden Camera), photo-

The Anne Frank house with its 1999 extension.

graphs that documented the sufferings of the people of Amsterdam even though it was strictly forbidden to take photographs outside the house. For example, a camera could be concealed under a coat and photos taken through a buttonhole.

When the Allies were repulsed at Arnhem in September 1944 the north of the Netherlands became isolated. In Amsterdam the hunger winter of 1944–45 took its toll in human lives. In order to obtain fuel the Amsterdammers stripped many empty houses, particularly in the Jewish quarter. The German army surrendered on 5 May and Amsterdam was liberated on 7 May 1945.

Gerrit van der Veen, a well known member of the resistance. He was executed in the dunes at Overveen on June 19 1944.

Mourning and Remembrance

Of the 80,000 Amsterdam Jews only five thousand survived the concentration camps. Amsterdam therefore lost ten percent of its population on all social levels. In 1946, to honour the February strike, Queen Wilhelmina bestowed the heraldic motto 'Heldhaftig, Vastberaden, Barmhartig' (Valiant, Resolute, Merciful) on the city. *De Dokwerker* (The Dockworker), a statue by Mari Andriessen in commemoration of the February strike, was unveiled in December 1952. The *Nationaal Monument* on the Dam (1956) honours all those who fell defending freedom in the 1940–1945 War. The Hollandse

The Canadian liberators were given a passionate welcome.

On June 28 1945, the third day of the official liberation celebrations, Queen Wilhelmina stood on the balcony of the Palace on the Dam to witness a great military parade. (GAA)

NH GRAND HOTEL KRASNAP
VERWELIUS BOUWEN

Schouwburg has been turned into a place of remembrance for all the deported Jews. The office and the back of the Frank family's house have been maintained as a place of remembrance.

The national Monument on the Dam, by John Radecker and J. J. P. Oud.

Statue of Anne Frank.

The limits to growth 1945–2002

Chapter 7

The opening of the Amsterdam-Rhine Canal, poster by Eppo Doeve, 1952. (GAA)

(p. 124)
Amsterdam's most recent expansion, IJburg. Drawing by A. J. Molenaar, Projectbureau IJburg.

After the Second World War Amsterdam had to renovate and expand Schiphol and the harbour, its main sources of prosperity, in order to make up for the backlog in housing and adapt to the demands of modern traffic. Schiphol grew into a large airport, which in the nineties was very close to the limits of its expansion. Those living in the vicinity and conservationists alike resisted the overflow of such a huge traffic centre.

Thanks to the North Sea Canal and the Amsterdam-Rhine Canal Amsterdam became both a Seaport and a Rhine-port. Therefore the harbour mouth and the locks in IJmuiden, plus the quality of the Amsterdam-Rhine Canal as far as the dam at Wijk bij Duurstede, are the subject of continuous concern to the city. An important advantage of the Amsterdam harbour is that from IJmuiden to Wijk bij Duurstede the water is at the same level. This is in contrast to Rotterdam where, although it does not have any locks, there are appreciable tides within the harbour. However, for the maintenance and improvement of both canals, Amsterdam was dependant on the government.

When the harbour entrance of IJmuiden needed enlargement a commission was installed by Mayor van Hall, which would then rapport to the government. His colleague in Rotterdam, G. E. van Walsum, strongly advised him to involve someone of the Ministry of Waterways and Public Works. In his memoirs van Hall wrote;

The Amsterdam Harbour-company.

'Although we Amsterdammers are always inclined to solve our own problems, we have taken up the advice of van Walsum'. After this the whole process was completed without any problem, and , in 1967, the harbour entrance with its peculiar asymmetrical shape was first taken into use. The fact that van Walsum's advice was needed is a good indication of how much Amsterdam was still turned into itself. One problem of the Noordzeekanaal is that it is only 15 metres deep where it flows across the Velsertunnel, something which, in the future, might cause a problem.

The harbour has moved, as had been provided for in the AUP, from the Eastern Harbour Area to new harbour basins to the west of the city; closer to the sea and without the inconvenience of the Hem bridge. In 1970 this process was completed. The Stoomvaart Maatschappij Nederland, which had lost its passage ships to Indonesia, co-operated with the Rotterdamsche Lloyd, which eventually led to a merger in 1969. Even then the Oostelijke Havengebied lay destitute. In the sixties the further expansion of the harbour in IJmuiden, plus the newly designed industrial area Noordzeekanaal met with fierce resistance form the environmental organisations.

The Western Garden Villages

In 1948 J. J. van der Velde became Alderman of Public Works. 'There was nothing in my office, save two copies of the General Expansion Plan of 1935', he said, 25 years later. 'I knew nothing of urban development but I read it in one go, throughout the night. I then called my chief of Public Works, and told him to start working straight away. "But Alderman", said he, "does the Hague approve?"' Upon which the little Alderman had answered: ' You do as I say and leave the political responsibility to me'. The chief new that the government, whenever rebuilding was concerned, gave priority to Rotterdam, which centre had been bombed on 14 May 1940, and the Hague, where a broad belt had been destroyed b the Germans, and the Bezuidenhoutkwartier had been bombed by the English. Amsterdam, which had lost ten percent of its population from al social classes, was of no political importance.

Amsterdam had to build. The sand that was needed to make the area ready to be built upon had to be won by sucking it away from under the layer of clay on the bottom of the Sloterpolder, creating the new Sloterplas., thirty metres deep. Long concrete piles were ordered, of which the transport and storage were costly. To quicken the process van der Velde ordered the piles to be driven into the ground before the licences to rebuild had even been granted by the Hague. When, subsequently, the Minister of Rebuilding summoned van der Velde to his office to explain this, he was told that the piles had been 'vertically stored', because horizontal storage was too

Alderman J. J. van der Velde in 1948, during the meeting on the General Expansion Plan. (Author's collection)

expensive and the piles would be damaged by children playing cops and robber on them. The minister chose to ignore the breach. 'A shame', the ex-Alderman explained, when at old age, he told his story. 'Would it not have been an honour to have been charged with fighting against housing shortage'.

The western garden villages and Buitenveldert were built according to a plan that stemmed from a different age. The new style of the Nieuwe Zakelijkheid was given a chance to realise its dreams: sun, well thought out mapping, storage for bikes and prams and a functional, conveniently arranged design. Unfortunately, they was not a lot of money, the motto 'we are rebuilding, everything is scarce' reigned. More often than not the fanciful details were scrapped by the red ink of a civil servant, which has led to a dull living area. Also, they had not foreseen such an increase in traffic in 1935. Because of the idea that traffic wasn't to interfere with living areas, the main traffic arteries were raised and free of junctions. In 1952 the

Housing, just after the Second World War.

Slotermeer was festively opened. Queen Juliana had tea and biscuits in the living room of one of the first inhabitants. In 1960 Amsterdam Noord got its own expansion plan.

All this did not lessen the housing shortage, so, in the sixties, Amsterdam designed the Bijlmermeer, a living area that could house a hundred thousand people. These were spacious apartments in huge concrete flats, in between which nature was spared. Al traffic lanes were raised. An old idealistic plan which derived from the twenties was brought into reality; people would feel a sense of freedom in a housing area in the middle of nature. This vision, however, was dated. The needs of the people and the problems of society had changed. The first Bijlmer flat was built in 1968, but the concrete high rises did not attracts enthusiastic occupants. The green areas became a haven for criminals. Meanwhile, the housing shortage increased faster than the council could build.

Modern traffic completion for Amsterdam West. (Vereniging 'De Amsterdamse Haven')

Traffic

In 1945 Amsterdam was practically unsuitable for modern traffic. The ferry behind the central station was the only means with which Noord or indeed Noord Holland. The Hague road hadn't been built yet, so all the traffic, whether it cam from Haarlem or the Hague, had to travel via the Munt. After the liberation the council saw a chance to tackle the traffic problem along with a few other things. At the Waterlooplein three traffic improvements would cross each other: the route of the future IJtunnel, a wide road through the Nieuwmarkt area to the central station and the underground, which would link the south-east of Amsterdam with the Central Station. Anotherbenefit was that the problem concerning the city hall could be solved. This could be built on the site of the old Vlooienburg, between the Waterlooplein and the Amstel. All the plans of the Public Works have been executed, save the road through the Nieuwmarkt, which was blocked by the protest group 'Nieuwmarkt' and other city-loving fellowships. The IJ tunnel was opened in 1968, the Weesperstraat and Valkenburgerstraat had been demolished. The construction of the underground was a new threat to the Nieuwmarkt. This lead to serious disturbances with the inhabitants in 1975. The underground was built, but extra care was taken when they rebuilt the Nieuwmarkt afterwards.

In the city as a whole traffic circulation was promoted by the construction of a bridge over the Vondelpark (completed in 1948), the Schellingwouderbrug in 1957 and the Torontobrug at the Amstel Hotel, which was only completed in 1969. The A-10 ring road, completed in 1990, finally promised to bring relief to the city. But it was the same story as with house building that could not keep pace with the housing shortage; all these measures failed to bring the desired relief.

Schiphol grew into a large airport, and was confronted with the boundaries of its growth in the nineties, when environmental activist and people that lived nearby started to protest against such a big airport nearby.

The Sixties

In the sixties, when prosperity increased due to pay increases, a sudden resistance against the civil services' policies arose. This discontent manifested itself via the Provo movement, who made fun of the hierarchies of the time. The youthful Provo's demanded a small-scale city as oppose to the large-scale technocratic ideal the council tried to establish. Was it necessary to keep building, to keep making way for traffic? The Provo's anticipated with horror that the traffic expansions would lead to the building of hotels, flats, shopping malls and offices in the centre of the city. However, prosperity would allow both the small-scale as the large-scale variant. In the midst of this turmoil the city-loving fellowships succeeded in halting the traffic expansion through the Nieuwmarkt. They pointed out the cultural heritage of the Huis de Pinto, Along the old sea-dike Antoniesbreestraat. In 1968 the Huis de Pinto was acknowledged as being a monument which needed restoring, and because of this strategic victory the structure of the old city was saved.

In 1969, the Jordaan, which had escaped redevelopment in the twenties, was next on the list. But the tide had turned. A new generation of young intellectuals and artists were now possessed with the dream of a small-scale city centre as a place to live. They believed that to keep on adjusting the city to the growing traffic was a bad development. The traffic had better adjust itself to the city. This new generation spread out to the Jordaan, where the slum houses were restored and often amalgamated into bigger houses. New life was breathed into the old working-class area. And where did they leave their car? Many young intellectuals traded their car for the delight of living in the old centre.

Amsterdam begot some world fame in the sixties as a haven for hippies and other back-packers. The people spoke of a 'magic centre', and a magical glow still shines on this period in the memories of many. The policy towards soft-drugs was mild in Amsterdam. The circle shaped and stepped National Monument had a magical effect on the often young tourists, who packed together and slept there. From 1967 onwards every Sunday, the Vietnam demonstrations, in which thousands of people demonstrated against the American war in Vietnam, played an important role in city life.

The plan for a gigantic city hall/music theatre at the Waterlooplein met with fierce resistance from those who adhered to small-scale building. Aldo van Eijck's Burgerweeshuis of 1960 was the epitome of small-scale architecture. The building wasn't one massif block but split up into several small compartments, inspired by a village of the Drogon-people, whom van Eijck had met on a journey through the Sahara. This was structuralism. Van Eijck became the guru of small-scale thinking.

The plan for the city hall was a long standing and controversial one. In 1962 the award winning 1936 plan, the city hall at the Frederiksplein, was cancelled. In 1969 the Viennese architect Wilhelm Holzbauer won the international prize quiz for the Amsterdam city hall, to be built on the site of the Vlooienburg. In 1979 the government threatened to refuse to make the necessary funds available. Holzbauer then suggested to combine the city hall with another long

Demolishing Kattenburg. (Photo Cor Jaring)

The city hall/music theatre by Wilhelm Holzbauer and Cees Dam

standing project, the Opera, which was to be built at the Ferdinand Bolstraat, on the grounds of the old RAI, also destined to be demolished. The government, which had initially blocked the build of the city hall, gave its permission to the 'combination-plan'. Holzbauer was forced to co-operate with Cees Dam, who had inherited the Opera assignment from his father-in-law, G. M. M. Holt. They had two very different characters, condemned as they were to work together. Contrary to what one would expect, the Viennese Holzbauer was the introvert and sober of the two, whilst Cees Dam mad an approachable and self-assured impression. The city hall/music theatre was first taken into use in 1986 (music theatre) and 1987 (city hall). The Okurahotel at the Ferdinand Bolstraat is a reminder of where the theatre was to have been built, for the Okura had chosen its location near to the future Opera. The Okura was duly compensated.

Urban Renewal-overspill

The conflict between the two views on city improvements, small-scale v. large-scale was played out against the background of two defining movements of the sixties and seventies: urban renewal and the demographical crisis.

The nineteenth century belt was nearly a hundred years old and desperately needed repairs. This was costly and the big investors subsequently sold their properties there. The repairs thus never happened, and so the urban renewal became the council's responsibility. The council's city development service maintained the traditional ideas of light, air and space. The late nineteenth century blocks in the narrow streets, with their steep stairs and no space between the facades at the back were thus to be replaced by broad streets and big housing blocks. These would have a decent space between the facades at the rear and the space inside would be increased. There were plans for demolishing 75.000 or even 100.000 houses, and they would be replaced by less houses, according to the following rule: demolish two blocks, rebuild one.

The council introduced the principle of overspill, something which was common practice in the urban renewal projects in England. Overspill worked as follows: the inhabitants of the overpopulated areas, next on the list for urban renewal, were placed on the outskirts of the city or in new towns. In the case of Amsterdam, overspill meant that the inhabitants of an urban renewal area were encouraged to move to a nearby town, such as Almere, Hoorn or Purmerend, or even further away like Zwijndrecht or Den Helder. The families with a moderate income were the ones to opt for overspill, for in the country they would have access to better housing and a spacious environment. Thus the city lost an important part of its energetic inhabitants with a great purchasing power. They had been a stabilising factor in the neighbourhoods, both socially and economically.

Demographic Crisis

From 1965 to 1984 Amsterdam experienced a catastrophic fall in the number of inhabitants. Before the Second World War the city had more than 800,000 inhabitants, a number that by 1964 had risen to 870,000. After 1964, however, the number fell steadily and reached its lowest point of 670,000 in 1984. This meant that the population of the city had fallen by 200,000, almost a quarter, in twenty years. The number 200,000, however, was a balance between profit and loss. Many more than 200,000 people had left the city. These were mainly families on an average income. In the seventies this number fluctuated around 40,000 per year. The newcomers, in contrast, were often young people and immigrants, groups with little income. In 1975, the year that Surinam became independent, almost ten thousand Surinamese came to Amsterdam. Many of them were completely unprepared for life in a strange environment with a cold climate. The number of people on social security benefits rose from 37,000 at the end of 1974 to 47,000 at the end of 1975, an increase of 25 percent. In the same period, moreover, the average occupancy rate fell greatly. This had fallen from 4.29 in 1922 to 3.32 in 1960, that is one person less in 38 years; in 1980 the average occupancy was 2.31, that is one person less in 20 years; the number fell to 2.06 in 1990. However absurd it seems, it remained a fact that more and more accommodation was required for a decreasing population.

The squatters' movement developed against this background. The accommodation of people who had left often remained empty for a long time, awaiting demolition or rebuilding. This process stagnated because of the conflict between the large scale and the small. Young people looking for a roof over their heads occupied the empty buildings. Eviction often led to widespread and uncontrollable riots and destruction.

Compact City

In 1978 the city council agreed on a program which looked upon the city as a place to live, as a 'compact city' and as a city which limited its traffic. From now on urban renewal was to take place in concordance with the inhabitants. Preservation and renovation was the new rule. Only if it was absolutely necessary would buildings be demolished. An inventory was made of the areas within the city which could be used as supplementary building locations. Alderman Jan Schaeffer gave house building a new impulse. Although overspill was sometimes still necessary, it was no longer seen as the best solution. Jan Schaeffer succeeded in starting up building once more. 'One cannot live in idle talk' was his catch-phrase. He said: ' Civil servants would call me up and say, "Mr. Schaeffer, that building plan, we would like to change something on the first floor". I used to reply: the roof is already built man!' In order to avoid evictions turning into riots, he bought up squats after which the squatters were allowed to rebuild them themselves, either into units for singles or for couples (Dutch: HAT). In 1984 Amsterdam saw its first rise in population. Squatting was reduced to what it should be, a marginal phenomenon.

The Oostelijk Havengebied, in which companies were no longer active, is one of the last complementary building locations to have been taken into use. Amsterdam followed e new planological procedure, where this large and complicated area was concerned. It had been the habit up till then to make up an end-plan for the whole area, especially an area this size. However, in the case of the Oostelijk Havengebied the deviated from this through process-planning. With process-planning a new plan was drawn up for each new segment of the area. This meant that one could keep up with the ever changing circumstances: different demands, technological improvements and architectural developments. Through the referendum of March 1991

The Amsterdam Harbour company, with its specialised container transport. (Photo Cor Jaring)

the population of Amsterdam chose for a low traffic centre in the spirit of their small-scale predecessors. The amount of parking spaces would be cut down drastically, and parking would become expensive.

Bachelor's flat by Jan Rietveld in Slotermeer, 1954.

Oranjes in Amsterdam

It was during the period of the Provo's and the squatters, this period of turmoil, that three very special days in the life of Princess, later Queen, Beatrix occurred: her visit to Amsterdam on the occasion of her engagement in 1965, her marriage on 10 March 1966, and her inauguration as Queen on 30 April 1980. These three days were ruined by riots. First there was opposition to her fiancé Claus von Amsberg, for he was German (Nobody could have foreseen that due to his modest and humane nature he would win the love of the people). However, the riots at the marriage and the 'crowning' were mainly an expression of protest about the housing shortage. In 1998 Beatrix celebrated her sixtieth birthday in the Palace on the Dam with her closest friends only.

The marriage of Prince Willem Aleander and Máxima Zorreguieta on 2 February 2002 was the first day of celebration for years without a discordant note. On that Saturday the weather was gloriously sunny. Burgomaster Job Cohen performed the civil marriage ceremony in the Beurs van Berlage. The Reverend Carel ter Linden consecrated the church marriage in the Nieuwe Kerk;

After the abdication by Queen Wilhelmina in September 1948, Juliana is inaugurated in the Nieuwe Kerk. On the balcony of the Palace Princes Wilhelmina shouts 'Long live the Queen' in honour of her daughter. (GAA)

The ten year old Princes
Beatrix greets the crowd
at the Dam. (GAA)

with a contribution from the Roman Catholic Father Braun. There was a national celebration the evening before in the Arena, at which the Orange fund was handed over as a wedding gift.

In 1980 Queen Juliana abdicates and Princes Beatrix is inaugurated. On the balcony of the Palace Juliana wishes her daughter well. (GAA)

KANTJIL & DE TIJGER
INDISC

(p. 140-141)
A tour in the Golden carriage on Prince William Alexander and Maxima Zorreguita's wedding day, February 2 2002. (GAA)

Decentralisation

Since 1978 the city has been gradually divided into boroughs. These boroughs have been given autonomy according to the rule 'all powers except a few'. Public transport, policing and taxation, for example, are among these few exceptions. These remained the responsibility of central city government. Osdorp and Noord were the first city boroughs; Amsterdam-Centrum was the last to be established (2002).

In order to achieve better spatial planning Amsterdam sought co-operation with a host of neighbouring towns in the 'Regional Organ Amsterdam, or ROA for short. There were plans to abolish the Amsterdam council, leaving the district council, the provincial council and the government. The people of Amsterdam felt as if their own city was to be abolished, and in the referendum of 1998 they overwhelmingly voted against this form of government. The city now remains constrained within its municipality borders, whilst modern times demand a bigger planning area.

Culture and education

When the city council moved to the Stopera, the old city hall, the Prinsenhof at the Oudewijds Voorburgwal, stood empty. The building is a collage of different fazes in Amsterdam history and contains a huge amount of (industrial)art. The council chamber dates from 1926 and was executed by Willem Penaat who made it into one coherent piece of art. It has therefore become a monument to the decorative arts that flourished during the twenties. Two separate pieces of art in the old city hall have had an eventful history. Chris Lebeau's murals form 1926 in the first-class wedding room consists of various allegorical apparitions, amongst which two heavily stylised nudes. On 24 February 1941 Alderman Boissevain ordered them to be taken from view. They were hidden behind jute wallpaper.

In 1953 Mayor d'Ailly was fed up with the fact that something was hidden in this room which, apparently, he wasn't allowed to see. He made a large cut in the wallpaper with his pen-knife. The murals were restore by Peter Alma.

The mural by Karel Appel from 1949, the 'Vragende Kinderen', had been hidden for a long time, in this case behind some panelling. The civil servants had complained about the painting, which confronted them with the simplified and elementary shapes of starving children. In 1959 the panelling was removed and the Vragende Kinderen was restored. When the building became empty, the council decided to make it part of the national heritage. The new inhabitant of the Prinsenhof, Hotel the Grand, has had the murals restored once more.

Amsterdam is the cultural and artistic centre of the country. Willem Sandberg, director of the Stedelijk Museum from 1945 to 1962, made 'Het Stedelijk' a worldwide concept. From 1948 onwards

The Palace on the Dam's Interior.

the painters of Cobra and the poets of the 'Vijftigers' group were active in Amsterdam. In 1947 Gerard Reve's De Avonden became a unique literary success. In the same year Anne Frank's diary appeared, with the title Het Achterhuis, and this became an unparalleled success world wide. The Stadsschouwburg was still the most important theatre in Holland. The Dutch Comedy by Guus Oster brought wide international repertoire. The sixties brought a group of people who wanted more engaged theatre. In 1969 this led to the Tomato-protest, in which protesters interrupted theatre performances by throwing tomatoes. For the performers, who were used to this treatment only by the nazi's, such a disturbance meant o total denial of the right to exist. It was the end of an era. In 1973 the Vincent van Gogh museum was opened in which the collection of Vincent van Gogh, Theo van Gogh's son was housed. Since the beginning of the

The Concertgebouw orchestra, conducted by Bernhard Haitink in 1965. (GAA)

Willem Sandberg, director of the Stedelijk Museum Amsterdam between 1945–1962. (Photo Ad. Petersen).

century the Stadsschouwburg had been the most important theatre in the country.

The National Ballet and The Dutch Opera, who shared the Stadsschouwburg with the Dutch Comedy, moved into the Music Theatre in 1987.

The capital is also a city of students. It has two universities and a concentration of higher professional training institutions.

The expansion of the Van Gogh Museum by architect Kisho Kurokawa, 1999.

Immigrants

The amount of immigrants from various countries increased rapidly. Next to immigrants from European countries, there came many Surinamese, Antilleans, Ghanese, Maroccans and Turks. Due to this the composition of Amsterdam underwent a huge change. Various complaints were to be heard amongst Amsterdammers., ordinary people, who had lived in Amsterdam all their lives without feeling any hate towards strangers. 'I do not recognise my own neighbourhood any more', 'You can smell grilled meat in the stairway all night', 'The boys upstairs pee in our garden' and 'my wife can't take it any more' were suddenly frequently heard complaints. Many people left their much loved working-class neighbourhoods.

On 4 November 1992 an Israeli aircraft with a full fuel load crashed in the South-east of Amsterdam. Two apartment blocks were destroyed in the resulting fire. This accident suddenly confronted the rest of Amsterdam with the fact that on the fringes of public and official interest a separate world had been created, with strange languages, marriage customs and cultural expressions, a world struggling with incomprehension, language problems and xenophobia. It turned out that a very large number of illegal immigrants also lived there.

Of the non-traditional religions Islam is by far the largest. They started out with improvised prayer rooms in existing buildings but, in 1985, the first mosque was built in the south-east of Amsterdam,

Bijlmermeer station, opened by Alderman Brautigam in 1971. (GAA)

Portuguese-Israeli Synagogue

the Taibah. In 1999 the Buddhists got their own temple on piece of land that had lain bare for ages at the Zeedijk.

Amsterdam has an old tradition of contact with waves of newcomers, such as the Ashkenazi and Sefardic Jews around 1600, the Hugenots around 1700 and the Chinese during the thirties, plus the constant stream of Germans from all layers of society. These newcomers all reacted differently. The Hugenots amalgamated with the people of Amsterdam, the only place they left their trace is in the Walenweeshuis and the Waalse Kerk. The Jews only became Amsterdammers in the Nineteenth century, but kept their own religion. They gave no offence. It wasn't a problem that the Jewish children didn't go to school on Saturdays and Jewish holidays. The Chinese remained a close community, they weren't really noticed. For the first time their has been a from of social recognition in 2000. Not only is there a Buddhist temple, there are plans for a Chinese area at the Oosterdokseiland, in concordance with the Chinese community.

The current problems concerning immigrants is once again a case unto itself. It is more complex and versatile than the examples mentioned above. This is because religious differences make assimilation and integration of certain groups difficult. The 'otherness' of the Islamic people gives offence, especially the position of the woman. Our traditional tolerance is too lazy, and does therefore offer no solution.

In this case there are two models of integration. On the one hand we have the segregation model, in which the minority is left isolated, until they have become self-conscious enough to be ready for integration. This is how, in Holland, the integration of the Catholics fared. Every group lived segregated, whilst the leader of the separate groups worked together heartily. The sixties melted away the divisions between the separate groups in society: anyone who can tell whether a certain TV programme is made by the NCRV or the KRO, is pretty smart. This model, a process that could take centuries, is too time consuming for the current problems. The other solution is the way of compulsory naturalisation. This would mean compulsory women's emancipation, compulsory amalgamation at school, supervision of education, language and citizenship courses, course money, examinations and fines for absence. This model could come into conflict with the constitutional and traditional rights of freedom of religion, education and expression. In reality no clear policy has yet crystallised.

The Taibah was Amsterdam's first specially built mosque.

The Latest City Expansion

The traditional harbour industries, such as shipbuilding and dry dock repair work, were lost in the seventies. Amsterdam no longer competes with Rotterdam, but is a medium-sized port with specialised services and container traffic. The economy sought power in new concentrations of offices, such as the Zuidas (South Axis), which since 1985 has expanded from the World Trade Centre (WTC) and curves from Zuid-Oost to Schiphol. In 1986 construction began on Teleport at Sloterdijk Station, an area based on the theme of telecommunications. On the Omval behind Amstel Station there are office skyscrapers surrounded by an expensive residential area.

Since 1997 the last solution for residential housing has been IJburg, built on artificial islands in the outer-IJ. Amsterdam, once closed off from the water by Central Station, would once again lie on the IJ. It appeared to be a marvellous plan, but the people of Amsterdam, who know the view from the Diemerzeedijk, did not trust it. In March 1997 a referendum on IJburg was held which the council won very narrowly. IJburg will be the last lobe of the city, as the north-eastern counterpart of the green lobe that is the Amsterdamse Bos. According to the plans this will be a modern, environment- friendly district. The design promises that we will not build any further into the IJ.

With IJburg, the limits of growth will be reached. There are only a few alternative possibilities within the existing city boundaries, such as building in great density, something which has already happened on the Sporenburg in the East Harbour Area; building across the A 10 ring road, as with the office building at the Bos en Lommerplein. Stacking functions, for example, an office block with a parking garage under it and a swimming pool on the roof, laying railway lines underground and building housing over them, are all possibilities to be considered. In around 2000 a start was made on transforming the western garden suburbs into the 'Parkstad' (Park city), in which the building will be denser.

In 2002 the Council-law was amended. A dualist system was introduced. The Aldermen no longer have to be chosen from the council, but can be recruited outside the council, form other councils even. The council has to make up its own agenda. Mayor Job Cohen, who was chosen by the government, has declared to be in support of a mayor becoming a democratically chosen official

The position of Amsterdam's most recent expansion, IJburg. (Projectbureau IJburg)

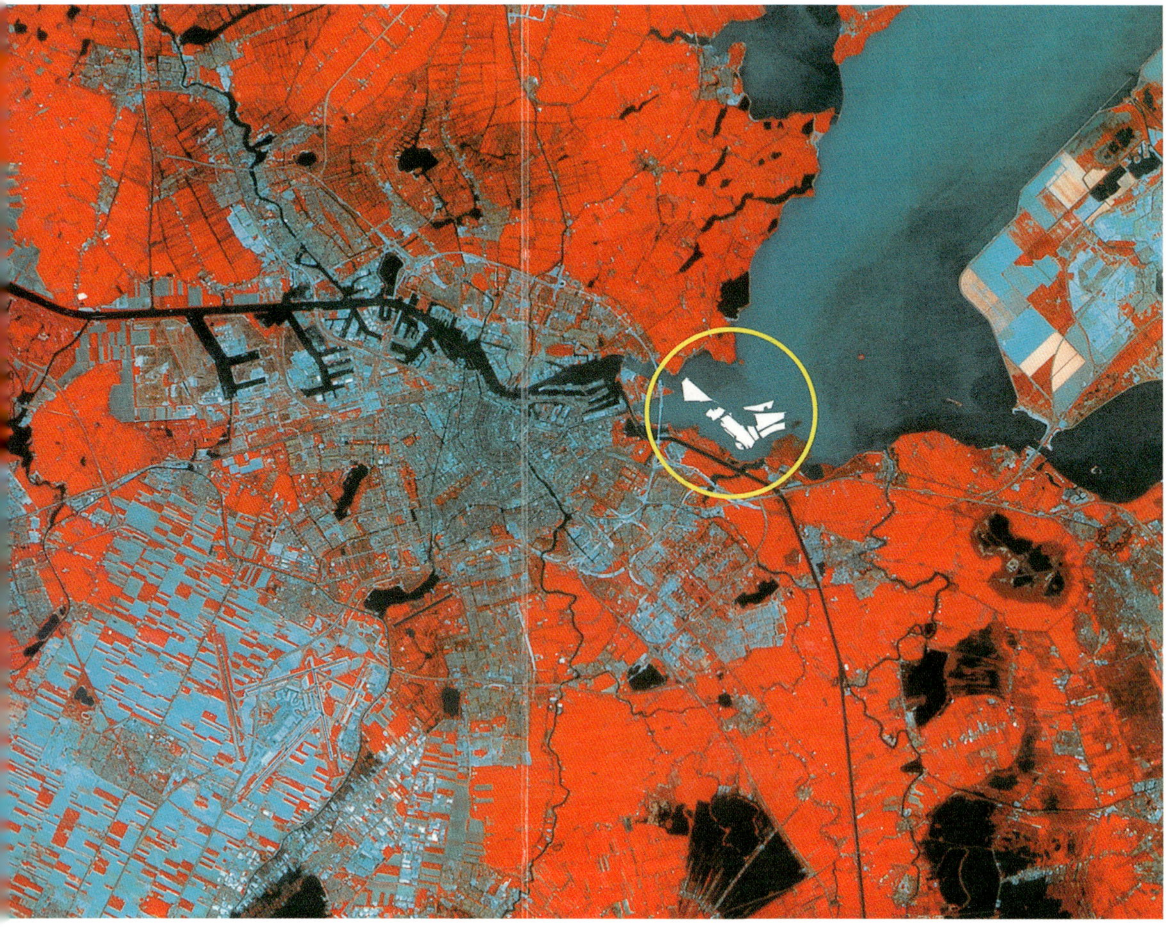

Amsterdam's Coat of Arms

Design by Georges Rueter. (Archief Stadsdrukkerij, Amsterdam)

Amsterdam's coat of arms consists of a red field, with a black vertical stripe in the middle. In this stripe are three silver St. Andrew's crosses. The St. Andrew's cross has four arms of the same length, which are all at a 90 degree angle. These crosses can be seen on the coat of arms of families and houses around the Vecht and Amstel area as early as 1300, in various different numbers and configurations. It is highly unlikely that they were meant as a tribute to Saint Andrew, who died a martyr's death on such a cross, for he didn't become known in this area until much later. One could compare the crosses with a brand, or licence plate.

The seal of Amsterdam showed only a ship as symbol for the sea-trade. It wasn't until 1419 that the ship is seen to carry Amsterdam's coat of arms with it's three crosses, as it is known to us today. The coat of arms is held by a lion. The three crosses were destined to become famous, they were a graphical success. The *crown* on the coat of arms came from Maximilian of Austria, son of the Emperor of Austria and heir to the throne. In 1489 the mighty city of Gent had taken him prisoner, and when he was released he was penniless. At this time Rotterdam and Woerden were rebelling against his authority. Amsterdam saved him from danger by lending him ten thousand Flemish pounds. As a reward, Amsterdam was given the right to the crown of Maximiliaan, heir to the throne of Austria, in eternal memory of his gratitude. This sounded good, but when the promise was made, the crown was no more than that of an *heir* to the throne. However, when Maximilian's grandson Charles V was crowned to be Emperor, Amsterdam did not hesitate to claim the crown for themselves, in order to increase their prestige. This is how it came to be portrayed on the Westertoren in 1631.

(p. 153)
The House of Bartolotti on the Herengracht.

Conservation of monuments and historic buildings

The Amsterdam city government is responsible for the maintenance of our historic inner city, the largest well-preserved pre-1800 municipal area in Europe. Amsterdam within the Buitensingelgracht is 802 acres large, of which 175 acres water and 627 acres land. The city centre contains around 8000 buildings which are listed as monuments by local or national government.

The Amsterdam inner city has always maintained its function as centre, the function as a meeting place, and source of inspiration for intellectual, cultural and economic modernization. One can detect a fluctuation in the use of canalside houses. They were once built as live- and storage house for the patricians, but since the twenties of the previous century the owners had gradually moved to more modern and cheaper housing in Zuid or Het Gooi. The Grachtengordel remained an attractive place to set up businesses and offices. During the sixties, however, many businesses found the centre to confining. The outskirts offered them ample parking and much better conveyance opportunities. All the newspapers, for instance, that had had their offices in the Nieuwezijds Voorburgwal were gone. Many deserted offices were squatted, such as the Grote Keyser, Keizersgracht 242-252, were the Technische Unie had had their office. And the Handelsbladgebouw on the Nieuwezijdsvoorburgwal, behind the Palace. When the squatting had died down many canalside houses and old warehouses were modernised and transformed into apartment, allowing them to become houses for living in once more. Sometimes one has to grudgingly accept the modernizations of an old building, like the penthouse with roof-garden on the van Beuningenhuis. A living city is to be preferred above a costly museum. It is in the interest of the buildings that they are used and reused constantly and in the process of which maintained up to scratch.

Throughout the centuries this old city centre has gone through a process of transformation, throughout which every period has left its marks. There are neo-gothic churches, fake-aged gables, French-reanaissance palaces (such as Herengracht 380, in which the NIOD resides), a modernised home (such as the famous Singel 428 of Abel Cahen, 1970)and on the Rokin 100, a sleek Jugendstil gable next to a sober neck-gable

The many infringements into the old cityscape have not damaged the original character of the canal facades, but we do seem to have reached the limits if we are seeking to maintain the old inner city. In 1999 the inner city was legally declared a protected cityscape. The surface of the protected cityscape is approximately 680 acres large, it doesn't completely match the surface of the city within the Buitensingelgracht. The best guarantee for maintenance lies in the intensive use of the inner city by its inhabitants, starting-up designers, publishers and events such as the annual Prinsengracht concert. The inner city is not a museum of facades, but simply an area of great splendour, which through its varied building gives one a birds eye view of the history of Amsterdam.

Amsterdam Canalhouses are since 2010 included in Unesco's List of World Heritage Sites.

RENOVATA
A° MCMLXXI
INGENIO ET
RELIGIONE ET
PROBITATE

DE VIER GEZUSTERS

(p. 154-155)
The Zandhoek.

The Amstel.

The Keizersgracht.

Important dates throughout history of Amsterdam

1275	Amsterdammers, belonging to Utrecht, get toll-privilege from Holland.
1300	First parish church, the Oude Kerk.
1303	Jacob van Aemstel occupies Amsterdam and turns against Holland. Amsterdam is punished heavily.
1306	Amsterdam gets city privileges.
1317	Amsterdam incorporated into Holland.
1345	The Miracle of Amsterdam.
1400	Right to choose it's own burgomasters.
1407–1467	Phillip of Burgundy rules over many provinces.
1408	The Nieuwe Kerk is founded.
1441	Amsterdam wins the battle with the Hanze-cities.
1489	Wins the right to carry the Emperor's crown in its coat of arms.
1515–1555	Belongs to the Habsburg Empire of Charles V.
1535	Anabaptist revolt.
1538	Birdseye-view painting by Cornelis Anthonisz.
1543	All Dutch provinces join Bourgondische Kreits, part of the German Empire.
1555	Charles V abdicates, Amsterdam now belongs to the Spanish-Habsburg Empire.
1578	Satisfaction and Alteration.
1579	Union of Utrecht.
1581	Spanish King Philip II renounced, the Republic is founded.
1602	VOC is founded.
1612	The Driegrachtenplan, leading only to the Leidsegracht.
1621	The WIC.
1606	Rembrandt born in Leiden.
1642	Rembrandt completes the 'Night Watch'.
1648	Peace of Munster, start is made on the city hall on the Dam.
1652	Conflict with William II, Amsterdam retreats.
1658	Driegrachtenplan expanded to the east of the Amstel, under the eye of Daniel Stalpaert.
1669	Disastrous year, expansion of Amsterdam is halted.
1672	Rembrandt dies.
1676	De Ruyter dies.
1678	Vondel dies.
1682	Plantage is set up.
1713	Peace of Utrecht.
1748	Doelist movement and the tax leaseholders revolt
1795	The Batavian Republic.
1806	Kingdom of Holland; Amsterdam is capital and seat of the King
1810	Empire of France.
1813	Amsterdam becomes capital under sovereign monarch.
1815	Capital of the Kingdom of the Netherlands.
1876	North-sea canal is opened.
1914	F. M. Wibaut become first social-democratic alderman (until 1931).

1917	H. P. Berlage's Plan Zuid accepted.
1935	Publication of the General Extension Plan.
1940	German occupation.
1941	February strike, protest against Jewish pesecution.
1947	Het Achterhuis and De Avonden are published.
1952	Slotermeer inhabited.
1968	First house in Bijlmermeer inhabited.
1969	Actie Tomaat against traditional theatre.
1978	City government chooses compact city.
2002	Changing of council-law.
	First houses in IJburg inhabited.

Terms of office of the Mayors of Amsterdam in the Twentieth century

1891–1901	S. A. Vening Meinesz
1901–1910	W. F. Van Leeuwen
1910–1915	A. Röell
1915–1921	J. W C. Tellegen
1921–1941	W. de Vlugt
1941–1945	[E. J. Voûte regeringscommissaris voor Amsterdam]
1945–1946	Feike de Boer, waarnemend burgemeester
1946–1956	Arnold J. D'Ailly
1956–1967	Gijs van Hall
1967–1977	Ivo Samkalden
1977–1983	Wim Polak Phzn.
1983–1994	Ed van Thijn
1994–2001	Schelto Patijn
2001–2010	Job Cohen
2010–	Eberhard van der Laan

Accountability

The publisher has endeavoured to accomplish the acknowledgement of the illustrations as completely as possible. Contemporary photo material mainly originates from the author and publisher's private collections. If any person claims the rights to missing or incorrect acknowledgements, please contact the publisher.

Abbreviations

AHM	Amsterdams Historisch Museum
GAA	Gemeentearchief Amsterdam
RMA	Rijksmuseum Amsterdam